A Moment in History

*The Story of the American Army
in the Rhondda in 1944*

Bryan Morse

First edition: 2001
Second edition: 2007
Copyright Brian Morse and Y Lolfa Cyf., 2007

ISBN: 978 184771 019 2

Printed on acid-free and partly recylced paper
and published and bound in Wales by
Y Lolfa Cyf., Talybont, Ceredigion, SY24 5AP
e-mail ylolfa@ylolfa.com
website www.ylolfa.com
tel 01970 832 304
fax 832 782

The thing that makes us come back though is that the people were so kind and willing. They gave us the keys and let us do as they would have their own sons do. Most of all the fellows in the Company have said that this was the best place they ever had except for home.

This is an extract from a letter written home while on leave by Pfc. Arthur Bonner dated March 13th 1945. Pfc. Bonner was a member of the 185 Port Company, 487 Port Battalion, U.S.Army.
He was billeted with Mr. and Mrs. Colin Exell of 41, Troedyrhiw Terrace, Treorchy, Rhondda.

To the people of Treherbert, the Rhondda Valley and the Welsh people. We are forever grateful for the moment in History you shared with us.

This is the inscription on the inside cover of the 186 Port Company's Unit History received from former GI. Karl Gaber living in Bulger, Pennsylvania, dated March 1999.
Pfc. KarL L. Gaber was a member of the 186 Port Company, 487 Port Battalion, U.S. Army. He was billeted with Mr. and Mrs. Thomas Jenkins of 88, Gwendoline Street, Treherbert, Rhondda.

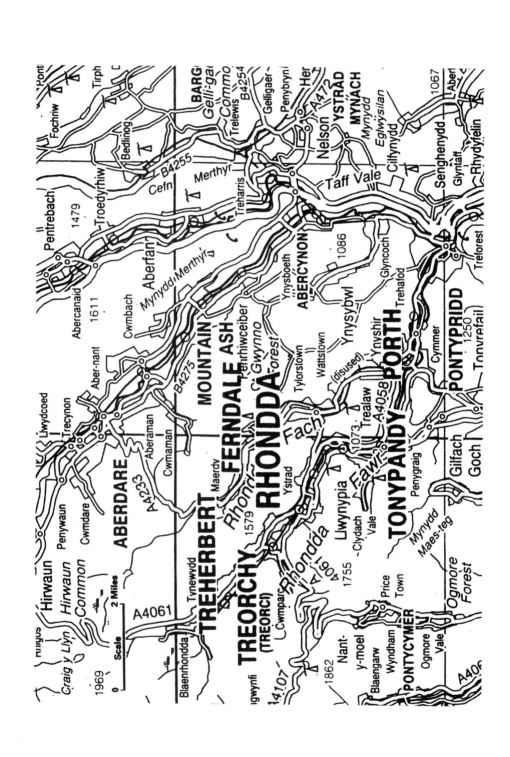

CONTENTS

ACKNOWLEDGEMENTS

I would like to thank:

The veterans and relatives of veterans who served with the 487 Port Battalion, the 517 Port Battalion, the 94th. Medical Gas Treatment Battalion and the 509th. Parachute Infantry Regiment of the United States Army.

The Rhondda Borough Public Library Service.

The Rhondda Leader.

The Trustees of the Welch Regiment Museum, the Castle, Cardiff, Wales.

The U.S. Army Military History Institute, 22 Ashburn Drive, Carlisle Barracks, Carlisle. Pennsylvania, U.S.A.

The National Archives at College Park, 8601 Adelphi Road, College Park, Maryland, U.S.A

The National Personnel Records Centre, Military Personnel Records, 9700 Page Avenue, St. Louis, Missouri, U.S.A.

Centre for Historical Research and Documentation on War and Contemporary Society, Residence Palace, Rue de la Loi, Brussels, Belgium.

American Battle Monuments Commission, 68 Rue du 19 Janvier, Garches, France.

Members of the Military Vehicle Trust, U.K.

I appreciate the assistance of Michael Morris of Penygraig for his invaluable help with the computer work.

Lastly, my most sincere thanks to my wife, Janis, for her support and encouragement.

INTRODUCTION

In 1944 I was living at 9 Gilfach Road in Tonypandy. Two American soldiers were billeted with my neighbours Mr. and Mrs. George Smith.

We shared a communal backyard with outside cold water taps. As an eight year old I was fascinated with these Americans and every evening I would sit on the stone steps and talk to them and watch them clean their equipment. When this was done they would wash and prepare themselves to go out for the evening.

Suddenly, to my great disappointment, they were gone. They had received orders in the early hours to report to their depots by 6a.m. to move out of the area. Later that morning Mrs. Smith came round to my house with a large parcel. They had left some presents "for the kid next-door". There was a letter to me, an Old Moore cigar box full of candy and gum, a pair of gaiters, a side cap, a helmet and a U.S. Army Bible. In the cover of the Bible was written "Presented to" then my name, address and the date, June 1st 1944. These items I valued greatly and have to this day.

For the kid next door

Fifty years later in 1994 great preparations were in hand to celebrate the successful D-Day landings in Normandy. Commemorative editions were promised in the local press and I hoped to learn something about the American presence here in the Rhondda in 1944. I was to be disappointed, there was no mention of them at all. There had been such strict wartime security that nothing about them had been recorded.

Making enquiries at some of the local Old Age Centres I discovered that not only had they been here in large numbers but had been billeted throughout both Rhondda Valleys. They were well remembered and with great affection. I resolved to try and uncover the events of those days. My research revealed a unique story.

The story is based on the memories of the people who lived through those historic times. It could not have been told without the generous co-operation of local people and former G.I.s and their families to whom I am most grateful. This is their story and one they did not wish to disappear unrecorded.

This is a factual account of the time. The Minutes of the Rhondda Urban District Council supplied the initial information. The Rhondda Leader, although strictly constrained by the need for military security, reported on reception arrangements and social events. This information was vital in recording the history of the period and shows the essential value of a local newspaper. The reports are reproduced in full to illustrate the efforts of local people and record the names of those who took part in these activities.

The American soldiers, the G.I.s, lived in the homes of local people and it is here that personal memories are strongest. With the passage of time, well over half a century, it is inevitable that many stories will remain untold. Films for private use were virtually unobtainable and the taking of photographs of military events was totally prohibited because of wartime security.

The reason for the American Army being billeted in the Rhondda was a closely guarded secret. The American forces were billeted in the Rhondda Fawr and Rhondda Fach and in the lower Rhondda extending to and including Pontypridd.

The Rhondda Leader in part of its editorial of March 4th 1944 announcing the imminent arrival of the American Army exhorts its readers to welcome them. "The friendly spirit is the duty of every person in the Rhondda remembering the words, I was a stranger and you took me in, Pontypridd is planning to do its part and we trust that all sections of the community will co-operate."

The American soldiers were arriving in a unique environment. The Rhondda Valleys world famous for its coal production was also famed for its hospitality. The welcome accorded to these G.I.s both in public and in private was tremendous. It was a credit to the Rhondda people of those days of which they could be justly proud. That the Americans appreciated this is evident in what was said and written by them.

Rhondda Leader September 16th 1944
Writing to Mr. and Mrs. Derrick, Charles Street, Tonypandy with whom he was billeted before going overseas Pte. Roger Klute of the United States Army stated that to keep fresh in the minds of the Americans who stayed in Tonypandy the excellent treatment they had received whilst here they called one of their trucks "The Tonypandy Special". Those who met Pte. Klute and his billeting partner are asked to accept their sincere good wishes and thanks.

Rhondda Leader September 23rd 1944
U.S. Thanks to Ferndale. Following are extracts from a letter received by Mr. and Mrs. Murnane, 88 Duffryn Street, Ferndale, from Sgt. Rocco Pardo, U.S. Army, and is typical of many received last week by Ferndalians.
Somewhere in France.

Hello to everyone. I am writing a few lines to let you know that I am feeling fine and hoping this letter will find you and the family the same. Lucas and I am getting along very well and we sure do miss you people. I am going to send you my home address. Am sorry I can't tell you much about France because I haven't seen much of it.

To tell the truth all the boys in the Company are always talking about Ferndale how nice the people were to them and God knows I sure do miss it too. Please let me hear from you. I often think of you as a family and would be glad to receive a copy of the Gazette.

Tell everyone in the good old town of Ferndale, Hello! from a little Yankee soldier Pardo. Lucas is still shy.

Extract from a letter written by former G.I. Pfc. Karl Gaber dated 31.7.00.
I try to imagine what your book is about. I think it must tell of the friendship that developed between the Welsh families and us young men, many of whom were away from home for the first time in their lives. You took us into your homes and hearts just like we were your own sons.

My aim was to uncover the story of the American Army in the Rhondda in 1944. I discovered the great bond of friendship that developed between the young American soldiers and their Welsh hosts which has stood the test of time.

The book reveals who these Americans were, why they were here and what happened to them in the campaigns in Europe.

Bryan Morse

CHAPTER ONE

The Historical Background

In June 1940 with France defeated and Dunkirk hastily evacuated Britain stood alone. A German invasion was feared and plans quickly put into operation to defend the British Isles.

Eighteen months later on the 26th of January 1942 the American invasion from across the Atlantic began to arrive in Britain. A month earlier the bombing of Pearl Harbour on December 7th 1941 had brought America into the war. By May 1944 there were over a million and a half U.S. troops, sailors and airmen in the U.K.

The Americans were not the only army in Britain. They were competing for space with the British Second Army of 1.7 million not to mention Allied contingents of whom 170,000 Canadians were the largest.

The lack of space caused all sorts of problems. The roads in Southern Britain were filled with vehicles. There were 104,000 American trucks and jeeps in addition to armoured divisions by March 1944. Men were harder to accommodate than vehicles. Accommodation required a mixture of existing British Army barracks and new construction.

As June approached vast tented encampments were set up. Less than 100,000 U.S. troops out of a final total of 3,000,000 passing through Britain were billeted in private homes, just 3% of the total.

The major part of Eisenhower's Expeditionary Force was concentrated in the counties of South and West England and also on a smaller scale on the southern coast of Wales which included Pembroke, Cardigan, Carmarthen, Glamorgan and Monmouth. On December 21st 1943 the total was 34,293. By 30th April 1944 the total had doubled to 68,877 and included Brecon. The Glamorgan total doubled from 15,919 on December 21st 1943 to 33,403 by April 30th 1944.

It was in this later statistic that the 4,000 Rhondda G.I.s come into the picture.

The journey from the United States to Britain was not without its difficulties as recorded by Pfc. Bernard Blumenthal, 186 Port Company, 487 Port Battalion. This Battalion was billeted in the Rhondda Fawr in May 1944.

An Ocean Voyage to Malpas, Newport. The 487 Port Battalion travels to Wales On August 4th 1943 to the tune of "Over There", a little fearful of what the immediate future had in store for us, we marched up the gang-plank of what was to be our home for the next fifteen days on the S.S.Cristobel. Damn glad to say goodbye to Camp Patrick Henry, Virginia's version of "The Black Hole of Calcutta". The luck of the 186 Port Company was running true to form. Again we had drawn the Joker in a full deck of cards. It seems we were one of the last outfits to board the Cristobel, so we drew the guest chambers, Compartment 4. Each Compartment held about two hundred and fifty men with gear. Here was the Joker, every bunk was taken by an Air Corps unit that had boarded the ship before us.

It seems that the Army higher-ups, hearing how rugged we were, had decided over the Cristobel that we would sleep in twelve hour shifts. Sleeping days and worrying nights. After what was beginning to look like "Bargain Day" in Maceys, we finally became settled.

Now we were ready to explore. After exploring until chow time we found out the following information. Our Compartment proved to be so far below deck, that literally speaking, we were to have nightly pinoche games with any stray fish that might happen to swim by. In addition Compartment 4 had our latrine, we discovered for about twenty men. Remember that latrine, it was to play an important par in our crossing

To top it off, the Cristobel turned out to be an ex-PanAmerican passenger ship converted into a troopship. Its normal carrying capacity was 1,500 people. But the Army and I think Colonel Jackson reached the same conclusion, that his boys could do and take anything that came along, which no one doubted.So we carried 3,300 poor souls, counting Officers and two dogs, who were to stand the crossing better than us as we were to find out a little later on.

By this time our stomachs told us it was time to eat, so still holding on to the tickets they had given us when we first came on board, we gaily tripped upstairs thinking to eat togethe. .So to our surprise all those with blue tickets would eat first.Ours were pink.

It seemed that eating consisted of sweating out a chow line for at least two hours. By the time you reached the head of the stairs leading to the galley below your spirit was pretty well crushed. Only one more obstacle to over come, when we found out what it was we shuddered, strong men wilted, faces paled if not already pale. Many showed their emotion by heaving in all directions faces paled, if not already pale. Many showed their emotion by heaving in all directions. You guessed it the odour coming from the galley below was unbearable. .

The next day we sailed and it seemed that we were heading due north. On our first day out and what proved to be a daily ritual we had boat drill which lasted an hour. It consisted of running upon deck to assigned places at the sound of a whistle wearing life jackets. Looking at those waves going up and down sure helped a fellow to be as sea-sick as the devil.

From the very first day out sea-sick or not, nothing could stop the card and dice games that were going on all over the ship.

Some of the boys did well. Tommy DiOrro for one, cleaned out one game making himself a few thousand dollars. By this time Tommy got sea-sick clutching his winnings in one hand he staggered off to his bunk, managed to get one shoe off, put his money on top of his shoe, dropped it to the floor and collapsed. Everyone around him was as sick as he was if not sicker. Nobody had the strength to reach out for the money on the floor.

By this time we had reached Newfoundland. At first everybody thought we were around Ireland. This was the 24th of August. We stayed there three days, long enough to repair some of the mechanical defects that caused one of the ships in our convoy to break down. On the morning of the twenty-eighth we pulled up anchor.

From here on in until we saw the mountains of Ireland, all that had gone before was a picnic compared to what was to come.

The evening of the twenty-eighth all hell broke loose. Picture three thousand men getting diarrhoea at the same time. The list of fellows brought down with diarrhoea and the heaves at the same time would fill a book.

With diarrhoea, a bad storm and two sub scares, we could say we never had a dull moment.

On September 4th after five days of storm, seven days of diarrhoea and nine days of sub scares we finally sighted the mountains of Ireland, they sure looked good to us. Not long after that we docked at Greenock, Scotland.

Before they they let us off the Cristobel on to the ferry that was to take us down the Clyde river to our train, a British General came aboard, made us a little welcome speech, thanking us for coming across and letting us know he had heard of our rough crossing. All we could think of then was if that guy doesn't stop talking soon we would cave in, our legs felt like rubber.

As usual it rained when we boarded the ferry. It didn't take us long to reach the quay where troop trains were ready to take us on the last lap of our journey. We made ourselves comfortable in the old fashioned coaches waiting for us. Soon card games were flourishing from one end of the car to the other. Nobody had any money left at this time so cigarettes were used instead.

By this time we had left Greenock behind us. Every place we passed it was the same thing, people waved like mad You would think we were going to win the war all by ourselves. It was our first glimpse at our British allies. Here was our first taste of that damp weather that characterizes Europe.

At every stop people waved and the boys kept throwing them cigarettes and candy

When we awoke twelve hours later we found ourselves pulling into the station of Newport, Wales. During the twelve hours we had travelled down from Scotland, through England and into Wales.

We disembarked at Newport, as usual it was raining. By now travelling in the rain had become a tradition with us. We wouldn't feel right if we didn't. Our legs still feeling wobbly, some one had got the bright idea of marching us to our new camp.

Off into the rain we marched, a better word for it was staggered. It was bad enough that our legs were wobbly, but they had to march us up hills and down hills. It was only a three mile march, but to the boys it felt like three hundred.

Finally, we came in sight of our new camp. Imagine our surprise to find that Camp Malpas was a camp in name only. It was a sea of mud. We just stood there in the rain. I remember some guy wise-cracking, "Three thousand miles to a mud hole."

However, on looking back, the boys agree that our trials and tribulations were a small price to pay for the gigantic task that lay ahead of us. It was not many months later that we were to learn that we had been selected to be part of General Eisenhower's task force that was to make the Invasion of France an overwhelming success. Yes, we were to be part of the magnificent First Army, a veteran Army made up of the cream of our Armed Forces.

Yes, you will admit there was a due need for getting us overseas as rapidly as possible. After all wars are won "By getting there Fastest with the Mostest.

THE RHONDDA IN 1944

The Rhondda in 1944 was still a great coal producing area. In wartime coal was essential to fuel the war effort. Pit head gear and the huge slag heaps presented a grim industrial landscape.

Into this valley came the young men from America. Nearly five years of war and decades of industrial neglect had given the Rhondda a drab appearance. There was of course no painting and decorating in wartime.

The majority of homes had no bathroom. The outside toilets were at the bottom of the garden as far from the house as possible. The houses were heated by open coal fires and although some houses had electricity many were still using gas lighting. Candles were still very much in use.

Food rationing was strictly enforced and items other than essentials non-existent. There were queues for everything imaginable from bread and potatoes to hair clips and torch batteries.

There was the Blackout. There was no street lighting and no light was to be shown from any house or building. Torches were allowed if there was no air raid. The torches were limited in size and power, in short supply and the batteries scarce and of poor quality.

This was the Rhondda the G.I.s came to, lacking in material comforts but with an abundance of good will.

INVASION THREAT

In 1940, the threat of invasion by Germany was a very real one. Extract from a Broadcast Talk given by Sir Hugh Ellis in the Home Service Programme at 9.20 p.m. on Wednesday, 5th of June 1940.

"Now, once more, we have before us the possibility of invasion and already extensive military preparations are being made, as many of you will have seen, to meet a possibility that cannot be ruled out. These are very wise precautions and the Government would be greatly to blame if such preparations were not taken."

Local Home Guard commanders were issued with a Government leaflet entitled "If the Invader Comes".

The Germans had to gain mastery of the air for an invasion to be successful. They were defeated in the Battle of Britain by the Royal Air Force and the planned German invasion was abandoned.

A wartime pill-box still guards the Hopkinstown Road as it leaves Pontypridd towards the Rhondda

BRITAIN STANDS ALONE

Extract from the speech given by Winston Churchill to the House of Commons, June 4ᵗʰ 1940:
"Even though large tracts of Europe and many old and famous States have fallen or may fall into the hands of the Gestapo and all the odious apparatus of Nazi rule, we shall not flag or fail. We shall go on to the end, we shall fight in France, we shall fight on the seas and oceans, we shall fight with growing confidence and growing strength in the air, we shall defend our island whatever the cost may be, we shall fight on the beaches, we shall fight on the landing grounds, we shall fight in the fields and in the streets, we shall fight in the hills, we shall never surrender."

Extract from Churchill's speech to the Canadian Senate and House of Commons at Ottowa, broadcast to the world December 30ᵗʰ 1941.
Speaking of the French Government's surrender to the Germans, he said, "I warned them that Britain would fight on alone whatever they did, their generals told the Prime Minister and his divided Cabinet. In three weeks England will have her neck wrung like a chicken. Some chicken; some neck."

This defiant comment resulted in a popular wartime song.

Penygraig A.R.P.
Lyn Williams, Trevelyan Wilson, Jack Llewelyn, Glyn Morgan, Not Known, Owen Jarman, Not Known, Not Known, Llew Williams, David Howells, Not Known, Llew Mainwaring, J.K. Williams, Steve Richards, Aubrey Llyod, Not Known, Elved Miles.

In every town and village there were detachments belonging to an organisation known as the A.R.P. The memebers of the A.R.P. were known as Wardens and had the powers of special constables. Amongst their duties htey watched for lights that might be visible by enemy aircraft and drew the attention of householders to any light that had not been properly obscured. No torches were to be used during an air-raid and cigarettes had to be extinguished. "Put that light out was a commonly heard phrase at this time.

Treherbert - a typical Rhondda Mining community in 1944
This view shows the pattern of terraced houses with the colliery in the
background and various chapels dotted about.

This mining town was home to th 186 Port Company of the 487 Port
Battalion. The three other Port Companies were billeted in towns and
villages further down the Rhondda Fawr. The four Companies of the
517 Port battalion were in Penygraig, Porth and in towns in the Rhondda
Fach. The mountains in the Rhondda were used as a training ground by
the 2nd and 28th Infantry Divisons of the United States Army as well as
the troops billeted in the Rhondda Valley itself.

You may like to recall the rations, *per adult, per week.* Our younger readers will be surprised at the small amounts!

Bacon and Ham:	4 oz. (100 g)
Meat:	to the value of 1s. 2d. (6p today). Sausages were not rationed, but difficult to obtain; offal was originally unrationed but sometimes formed part of the meat ration.
Butter:	2 oz. (50 g)
Cheese:	2 oz. (50 g)—sometimes it rose to 4 oz. (100 g) and even up to 8 oz. (225 g)
Margarine:	4 oz. (100 g)
Cooking fat:	4 oz. (100 g) often dropping to 2 oz. (50 g)
Milk:	3 pints (1800 ml) sometimes dropping to 2 pints (1200 ml). Household (skimmed dried) milk was available, I think this was 1 packet each 4 weeks.
Sugar:	8 oz. (225 g)
Preserves:	1 lb. (450 g) every 2 months)
Tea:	2 oz. (50 g)
Eggs:	I shell egg a week if available but at times dropping to 1 every two weeks. Dried eggs—1 packet each 4 weeks.
Sweets:	12 oz. (350 g) each 4 weeks.

In addition, there was a monthly points system. As an example of how these could be spent, the 16 points allowed you to buy one can of fish or meat or 2 lb. (900 g) of dried fruit or 8 lb. (3·6 kg) of split peas.

Wartime Rationing (Courtesy of Woman's Weekly)

CHAPTER 2

The Story Begins

December 8th 1943

The American Army is coming to the Rhondda. This remarkable news was broken to members of the Rhondda Urban District Council at a meeting in the Council Offices in Pentre in the Rhondda Fawr. An extraordinary meeting had been called but this in itself was nothing new.

The fifth Christmas of the war was just two weeks away and there had been many emergency meetings before. To the normal mundane tasks of the Council had been added all the wartime regulations. The billeting of over 15,000 evacuees from the Blitz in London and the Midlands in 1940 had been the biggest task, the bombing of Cwmparc and the loss of life in 1941 the most tragic one. The news that the armed forces of the United States were coming to the Rhondda could only mean one thing; the long awaited Second Front, the invasion of Hitler's Fortress Europe could not be far away.

There was great excitement within the Chamber, the individual councillors vied with one another to offer suggestions to help cope with the arrival of the troops. The discomfort of sitting clad in their overcoats in the unheated Chamber was forgotten as they discussed the various options until late in the evening. There was one note of discord. With the memory of the Tonypandy Riots still fresh in many minds, the possibility that troops might be billeted in private homes caused great disquiet.

In 1910 Winston Churchill was the Home Secretary in Asquith's Liberal government and sent troops to the Rhondda to help restore order. It was resolved that whereas every effort would be made to co-operate with the Government the question of troops of whatever nationality being billeted on private citizens was to be resisted.

The Minutes of the Council Meeting on December 8th 1943 and a further meeting on January 12th 1944 record the bare facts and the Government's response.

Rhondda Urban District Council Minutes December 8th 1943.
The Clerk reported that he had communication with the Welsh Board of Health relative to the billeting of American troops in the Council area and informed the Board of the accommodation available in hotels and other places; that the Board had replied that they were faced with the necessity of billeting large numbers of American troops in the near future and it was proposed to billet two thousand in Rhondda, that the billets were required for lodging only, as feeding centres would be provided by the Military Authorities and asking for the co-operation of the Council and inhabitants in the matter and further stating the question of utilising alternative accommodation was receiving the attention of the Military Authorities but such accommodation would be supplementary to the billeting of such troops.

The Council having considered the matter it was resolved:
l. That the Clerk be instructed to make further representations to the Board for the billeting of troops in hotels and other suitable places and not in private houses.
2. That on the arrival of the troops, the Chairman and the Clerk be authorised to make the necessary arrangements for extending to them a welcome on behalf of the Council and residents of the Rhondda.

Rhondda Urban District Council Minutes January 12th 1944
American Troops Billeting. The Clerk reported that further representations had been made to the Welsh Board of Health regarding the proposed billeting of American troops in private homes in the district and a reply received stating that the representations had been noted and pointing out that the issue was one for the Military Authorities, who after investigating possibilities had decided that this particular contingent of troops should be accommodated in private dwelling houses.

R.U.D.C. Meeting 12th January 1944
The Clerk reported the receipt of a communication from Mr. J. Thomas No. 14 High Street, Treorchy applying on behalf of the Entertainments Section of the Anglo-American Reception Committee for the temporary use of the requisitioned Church Buildings at Conway Road, Treorchy and stating that it was intended to apply for the use of the Girls Club at Ystradfechan Field as a welfare centre for the American troops and it was necessary to be able to offer the Girls Club an alternative temporary building and that the building at Conway Road appeared suitable for the purpose.

There was a regular supply of information in the local press to keep the general public in touch with what was going on.

Rhondda Leader February 26th 1944
Penygraig – News in a Nutshell
Penygraig social circles are making active preparations to welcome Allied troops in the district.

BILLETING

Under wartime regulations the billeting of troops in private homes was compulsory. The actual billeting was the responsibility of the police. A house with a spare room had to accept a serviceman.

There were exceptions on the grounds of ill-health or if a woman lived in a house with no male present. The billets were required for accommodation only. Emergency feeding and washing stations were set up and special Nissen Huts constructed.

The actual billeting process aroused great interest. Large two and a half ton G.M.C. trucks would rumble into the streets carrying the American soldiers. Seated with the driver would be the local policeman, he would consult his list and allocate the G.I.s to their billets. Carrying their kit and personal belongings they would be introduced to their hosts. In some cases they brought their weapons with them. Mr. Spencer Jenkins had two G.I.s billeted with his family in Salem Terrace, Llwynypia and recalls "I looked into their room and they had what looked like two Bren guns on their beds."

As a general rule American officers were billeted in the homes of professional people such as lawyers or doctors. These better class homes would have bathrooms, phones and a degree of comfort and sophistication far removed from the more humble working class homes of the majority of Rhondda's inhabitants. The Enlisted Men, the ordinary soldiers, stayed in the terraced homes of the workers many of whom were miners.

Extra beds were required in some billets. The beds arrived in folded form at central depots. John Skinner remembers the arrival of the trucks at St. Barnabas Church, Penygraig. Huge piles were stacked on the church green with troops busily arranging their disposal to local homes.

CHAPTER 3

Initial Preparations

News of the imminent arrival of American troops spread like wildfire through the Valleys. A Council of Churches was set up to organise the preparations and committees formed in the various wards. Meetings to organise reception committees were packed with enthusiastic volunteers. Something big was in the air and local people felt driven to do their small part in organising the preparations for the long awaited Second Front.

Military camps were mushrooming in various parts of the country and the huge stockpiles of military equipment and the large scale movement of troops all pointed to the inevitable day when we and our allies would strike the final blow to rid Europe and the world of the tyranny of the Hitler regime.

The people of the Rhondda had sons, brothers, daughters and husbands in the armed services. Britain was now in the fifth year of the war and they had lived with the anxiety and gnawing fear for their safety over that period. Many Rhondda servicemen and women had lost their lives, been wounded or taken prisoner. The Rhondda Leader carried a continuing toll of casualities in their weekly editions.

Now the American boys were coming. They were thousands of miles from home and their loved ones and facing an uncertain and dangerous future. The people of the Rhondda were determined to give them every welcome.

The enthusiasm and unstinting effort put into this welcome is evident in the reports carried by the Rhondda Leader over this period.

Rhondda Leader January 15ᵗʰ 1944
To welcome Allied Forces... Cwmparc and Treorchy Preparations
*   Once again Ward 2 is the first in the field to form a reception committee for the Allied Forces shortly to be stationed locally and supplies proof of the endeavour to return the hospitality our lads in America are receiving.*
*   A meeting with this object in view was held at the local boys club. Its convener was Lt. Col. John Evans J.P. supported by Police Sgt. Moore. No step has been*

overlooked to organise the traditional hospitality of the district combined with every effort to make the stay of the Americans a happy and memorable one. At all the very enthusiastic meetings representatives of all public bodies and various services drew up a program which other wards could do well to copy.

At the helm of the affair are Mr. E.D. Wilde (Chairman), Major D.J. Thomas (Vice) Mr. John Thomas, Estate Agent (Treasurer) with T.J. Jenkins and T. Joseph Jones as joint secretaries.

The Entertainment Committee. Chairman Mr. Tom Llewelyn and Secretary Lt. J.A. Hickerton. They will be responsible for arranging dances, whist drives and light entertainment. A varied and attractive programme has been arranged. Sports Committee. Chairman Mr. T. Hughes, secretary Mr. Idris Rees. The committee will arrange for all the indoor and outdoor games. Already it reports that much progress has been made.

Musical and literary committee. Chairman the Rev. D.C. Rowlands B.A., B.D. secretary Mr. H. Dudderidge who will organise concerts, community singing etc. To this committee has been left the duty of arranging a reception upon the troops arrival. It will take the form of a public meeting at the Pavilion Cinema (kindly lent) on the first Wednesday after their arrival over which Councillor Iorweth Thomas will preside and an official welcome accorded by Lt. Col. John Evans J.P. and Mrs. Levi Phillips (Ystradfechan).

Selections will be rendered by the Parc and Dare Workmens Silver Band (Bandmaster Mr. Hayden Bebb) and the Treorchy Royal Welsh Male Choir (Musical director Mr. Gwilym Jones). There will also be community singing.

Every detail allotted to the sub-committees has been attended to with excellent results. It is very certain that our American guests will appreciate all this done on their behalf and will take back with them to the States memories and proof of the traditional hospitality of the Welsh mining folk.

Officers and members of these sub-committees are men rich in public service and under their guidance it is not to be wondered why the scheme will prove a hundred per cent success. Further reports of later arrangements will be given shortly.

The expected arrival of the Americans resulted in a great flurry of activity and then there was a lull. The committees had been set up and halls and chapels had been booked for the receptions. Bands, choirs and singers put on standby and then there was a period of waiting. The weeks passed into months and still the great influx of troops did not materialise. Nothing appeared to be happening.

However behind the scenes plans were being put into operation. Administrative details planned many months earlier were already being carried out. Small groups of American officers arrived early in January 1944 using the ordinary train service and staying in local hotels. Meetings were held with local government officials to formulate plans. Some local church halls were requisitioned namely St. Barnabas and Llanfair church halls in Penygraig and St. Dunstans Church hall in Ferndale were selected. These were used because they were constructed of timber clad with metal sheets and could be adapted for use as cookhouses. The more substantial stone structures were not a practical proposition since a water supply had to be installed for washing and toilet facilities and cooking stoves set up in the halls. Rhondda residents caught occasional sightings of large American trucks with their canvas hoods hiding what they were carrying, negotiating the narrow streets and steep hills. Small groups of American soldiers carried out the conversions, built small extensions and installed stoves.

The problem of feeding over two thousand troops could only be solved by building extra feeding centres. The erection of Nissen Huts provided the answer. The Nissen Hut well known to hundreds of thousands of British servicemen was a structure which became a familiar sight everywhere a building was required quickly. It was a temporary structure but was capable of being built strong enough to serve as accommodation or storage. It could be sited virtually anywhere and was easily camouflaged.

Nissen Huts were erected on land adjacent to the Rink Dancehall in Porth and lower down the slope from the Tin Chapel at the end of Leslie Terrace in Llwyncelyn. The Tin Chapel served as a dining hall. Both of these Huts were used as cookhouses. The present day Porth Library was then two empty shops and these were used as a foodstore by the United States Army. Another Nissen Hut was constructed on land adjoining Zion Chapel, Llwynypia, now the site of the Kwik Save store. Further up the Rhondda Fawr a Nissen Hut was built to the rear of the Pentre Legion. The food was cooked there and served in the large hall in the Legion itself. In Treherbert on land adjacent to the Cymric Club at the end of Taff Street, a further Hut was built to serve as a feeding station and cookhouse. The Cymric Club was also used by the American troops.

Over two thousand troops were expected and these had to be fed. The amount and quality of food provided for the British citizen was considered too little and too inferior by the American authorities for their soldiers. In addition, it was lacking in variety and there was no fresh fruit such as oranges and grapefruit. The American troops had two main gripes when they first arrived in Britain, the weather and the food. The first the Americans could do nothing about but the second they could solve. They saw to their own feeding arrangements. Huge quantities of food were imported through Cardiff and Barry Docks to feed the troops based in Glamorgan. It was ferried in trucks not only to the Rhondda but also to the camps set up in Bridgend, Porthcawl and elsewhere.

The food for the American forces was of such quantity, quality and variety compared with the meagre rations of the local inhabitants that it aroused some hostility and gave rise to the "overfed" jibe. A great variety of canned products were available, canned meat and fruit, canned fruit juices as well as dried and fresh fruit. Oranges and grapefruit were available which had long disappeared from our fruit stalls and bananas were totally unknown to the younger children. The Americans found our coarse wartime bread uneatable and produced their own. A huge bakery was set up under canvas in the Dunraven Park at Southerdown. Here they baked bread using white flour imported from the United States. It was supplied by trucks to all the areas covered by the South Western Command which included all of South Wales as far as Pembroke and Bristol and the South-West of England including Cornwall, Devon and Dorset.

There were daily deliveries using the large G.M.C. two and a half ton trucks, before the days of motorways, no Severn Bridges and negotiating the narrow country lanes. It must have been some drive.

British coffee at that time was Camp Coffee made from chicory that the Americans found undrinkable and so imported vast amounts of coffee beans. These were roasted and ground at the Southerdown site before being distributed elsewhere.

All this movement of foodstuffs required a great deal of organisation and manpower and involved a large number of trucks for its distribution. This aroused some criticism from the British Authorities.

In the Rhondda the main food store and distribution point was the old Town Hall in Dunraven Street which is the main street in Tonypandy. Older residents can remember as many as twenty to thirty trucks unloading at any one time.

Working parties of American soldiers were here early in the year of 1944. The Minutes of the Ton Pentre Conservative Club reveal the presence of the United States Army and also the value of money in those days. An extract from the Minutes dated February 9th 1944 under the heading Correspondence reads:

Appeal from Bristol Infirmary for the annual donation of £1 moved and carried. Appeal for a donation by Glyn Wales, County Councillor to support the American troops when they arrive for a night function. Moved and carried that we grant them £1 for the said occasion.

A report of that night's function was carried by the Rhondda Leader.

Rhondda Leader Report Saturday March 18th 1944
American Invasion. More than 150 American soldiers invaded Ton Pentre Conservative Club on Saturday evening March 11th as the guests of the members and Committee.

This was the first visit of such a large number of Allied troops and the Doughboys thoroughly enjoyed what they called true Welsh hospitality. Indeed they could have not been given a better welcome anywhere in the country than that accorded on Saturday at Ton Pentre.

The President of the club Mr. Harold Davies extended an official welcome to the Americans and wished them all a good evening's entertainment. Mr. Tom Davies (Club Chairman) also spoke and a concert was held in honour of the visitors.

Items were contributed by Messrs. Jack Davies, Ivor Thomas, Jack Meyrick, W. Owen, Len and D. Davey and W. Phillips.

Among the Americans who contributed to the entertainment were Sgts. Newman and Saunders and Pte. Simpson who sang "Mandalay".

The visitors paid high tribute to the club and to the Steward and Stewardess and their family.

The Steward and Stewardess were a Mr. and Mrs. Joyce.

The Minutes for March 14th Record:

Moved and carried that we pay Tom Thomas and Ivor Davies 8/- each (40p) for waiting Sunday, the night the American troops were here.

CHAPTER 4

Salute the Soldier Week

During April 1944 the Rhondda Council organised the area's "Salute the Soldier Week". These were campaigns encouraged by the Government to raise money for the war-effort through various forms of National Savings.

Events were planned throughout the Valleys. The American Army played its part. It provided military detachments for the parades and took part in the many social activities.

The "Week" lasted from April 22nd to April 29th. The newspapers carried adverts from local businesses sponsoring the events. There were tickets sold for a competition to guess the final figure raised. Although the campaign had a serious purpose a carnival atmosphere was engendered with various competitions, variety shows and dances.

Salute the Soldier Week opened with a series of parades. These were fully covered by the Rhondda Leader which is the source of this report.

The main opening ceremony took place at Pentre with a military parade outside the Council Offices on Saturday April 22nd. It took place in front of a distinguished assembly which included Sir Gerald Bruce, Brigadier-General R.E. Kane O.B.E. M.C., Lieut.-Colonel Nickelson (American Army) and W.H. Mainwaring M.P.

The same day saw the opening ceremony for Ward 11 (Maerdy, Ferndale and Blaenllechau). The public showed their interest by displaying flags and bunting and Ward 11 was really in holiday mood.

The parade which consisted of the Home Guard and all the civic organisations of the district together with a contingent of the United States Forces was one of the most impressive ever seen in the district. The Maerdy contingent marched to join the main parade at Ferndale and then proceeded to Darren Park, Ferndale where the opening ceremony was performed by Lieut.-Colonel Nickelson U.S.A. Forces who took the salute.

The Lower Rhondda Salute the Soldier Week commenced with a grand parade of service units and other organisations on Saturday April 22nd. The parade assembled at Wattstown Memorial Park and the opening ceremony was performed by Mr. W.H. Mainwaring M.P. Parade Marshalls were Major R.H. Pugh M.C. M.M. and Police Inspector Jack Pugh.

The parade moved from the Wattstown Memorial Park to the Cenotaph in Porth. Here the salute was taken by Captain F.J. Baly M.C. R.A. Standing with Captain Baly was Major Bunker Commanding Officer of the American detachment.

The parade moved along a pre-arranged route to the dispersal point at North Road, Porth. Large crowds lined the route and the parade proved most entertaining and picturesque.

Alf Richards of Porth was a member of the Home Guard unit in this parade. He recalls he was not impressed by the marching ability of the G.I.s. The Home Guard unit was trained by a Bill Rowlands who had been a Colour Sergeant in the Welsh Guards in the First World War: "We were trained like guardsmen," remembers Alf. "The Americans marched in a curious silence with their rubber soled shoes which contrasted with the steady tramp of the hobnailed boots used by British troops. Neither did they swing their arms and marched along in a casual manner with the occasional wave to the crowds lining Hannah Street."

LORD MAYOR ADDRESSES ASSEMBLY

A joint gathering of Home Guard, Civil Defence, A.T.S, a detachment of the U.S. Army and pre-service units headed by the Cory Bros. Workmens Silver Band paraded at Ton Pentre on Tuesday April 25th when Wards 3 and 4 comprising Pentre, Ton, Gelli and Ystrad held their Salute the Soldier demonstration. Thousands of people lined the streets as the imposing parade moved along the route to a position near the Indicator outside the Crawshay Bailey Office, Ton Pentre, where a salute was taken by Alderman Frederick Jones J.P. Lord Mayor of Cardiff.

Following the parade a meeting was held in Jerusalem Chapel, Ton, where several notable personalities addressed the assembly.

Colonel Birch who had seen service with the Eighth Army said it would be useless if we won the war only to find ourselves financially rocky. Therefore it was not only to lend money to purchase armaments to win this war that these savings campaigns were organised but also to stabilise our financial future.

The Lord Mayor intimated that he considered it to be a great privilege to address the meeting and he derived considerable pleasure in doing so, appealing to the Rhondda people to top the target of £300,000 and possibly reach £400,000. He observed that this country was the finest in the world and the present savings campaign might be the last required of the people of this country.

Captain H. Dressner of the U.S. Army remarked that when he came to this country first he discovered the most important thing in Europe and that was a warm welcome. Another American who spoke was Captain Reich, Chaplain to the U.S. Army. Mr. Sidney Tapper Jones, Town Clerk of Cardiff, who is a native of Pentre expressed confidence that the people of the Rhondda would top the target.

A civic reception was accorded the Lord Mayor at the Council Chamber, Pentre during the afternoon where he was formally welcomed by Councillor Frank Williams J.P. and other members of the local authority.

The edition of the Rhondda Leader dated May 13th, 1944 gave the result of the competition to guess the total amount raised by the savings campaign. It was won by W. Peckner of the U.S. Army with a nearest estimate of £413,OOO. The winner and runners up were informed they can claim their awards from the secretaries Mr. J.E. Williams 12, The Parade, Porth or Mr. W. Griffiths, The Vogue, Hannah Street, Porth.

To start the week's social events in Treorchy a dance was held at Polikoffs factory. Music was provided by an American Army danceband led by Pte. J.J. Jamaccio.

Alfred Polikoff Ltd. was a factory opened by Lord Nuffield at Ynyswen in 1939 making men's and boy's clothing. When war broke out the factory switched to the production of uniforms.

The large canteen had been kindly lent for the purpose of the dance and suitably decorated with flags and bunting. The assembly included Lt. Col. Mills O.B.E., M.C., Col. Nickelson U.S. Army and fifty American soldiers.

During the evening certificates were won by Mrs. Reed, 40 Clarke Street, Treorchy, Mrs. Jones 26 Ynyswen Road, Treorchy and Mr. Albert Tidy 11a Lower Alma Street, Pentre.

A Salute the Soldier address was given by Lt. Col. Mills during one of the intervals.

One of the events in Tonypandy was a soccer match between the R.A.F. and a Mr. Joe Fisher Xl at the Mid-Rhondda Athletic Ground. The match was followed by a dance held in Judges Hall, Trealaw. It featured the same American Army danceband which had entertained the dancers in Treorchy earlier in the week.

A grand and unforgettable climax to Mid-Rhondda's Salute the Soldier celebration was the Radio Bee at the Central Hall, Tonypandy on Saturday April 29th. The show was organised by Messrs. Jack James, Penygraig and Bert Evans, Oxford House, Tonypandy.

Skillfully arranged each item was breezily announced by Messrs. Jack James and Bert Evans, Mrs Jack James and Miss Mendicott and Mr. Herbert Jones in turn earned loud applause from a crowded audience.

The programme consisted of items by the famous band of the Welch Regiment. (Conductor Mr. T. Clegg by kind permission of the officer commanding).

The show followed a pattern of a radio broadcast bringing together a collection of well known shows:

Bandstand. Trans-Atlantic Call featured Pte. Bill Geary from California, a member of the U.S. Army.

News Bulletin. I Want to Be an Actor, an item which attracted several aspirants.

S.O.S. Youth takes a Bow featured members of the celebrated Blaenclydach Junior Orchestra, Miss Mair Edwards, Clydach Vale (Soprano) and Miss Elizabeth Naughton Evans, Tonypandy (elocutionist).

The Week in Westminster with a commentary by Mr. Will John M.P.

Saturday Night at Eight entitled "Into Battle, an American Commentary" was given by Major Young of the United States Army. Music While You Work was performed with appropriate selection by members of the Williamstown Gleemen with Miss Mary Carpenter at the piano. Other items followed, in Town Tonight, The Week's Good Cause, a Spelling Bee and an Order of the Day.

These items were followed by a Grand Tableau entitled Salute the Soldier. A tableau in which members of the Armed Services both male and female from the Army, Navy and Air Force together with representatives from the U.S. Army stood under the flags of the Allied nations. This display was accompanied by music of the Band of the Welch Regiment and a selection by the male octet.

Messrs. Jack James and Herbert Jones effectively made the final commentaries.

The effective lighting arrangements were by Messrs C.R. Springsguth and E. Isaac, Tonypandy.

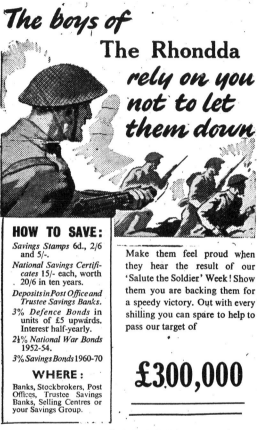

The boys of The Rhondda rely on you not to let them down

HOW TO SAVE:

Savings Stamps 6d., 2/6 and 5/-.

National Savings Certificates 15/- each, worth 20/6 in ten years.

Deposits in Post Office and Trustee Savings Banks.

3% Defence Bonds in units of £5 upwards. Interest half-yearly.

2½% National War Bonds 1952-54.

3% Savings Bonds 1960-70

WHERE:

Banks, Stockbrokers, Post Offices, Trustee Savings Banks, Selling Centres or your Savings Group.

Make them feel proud when they hear the result of our 'Salute the Soldier' Week! Show them you are backing them for a speedy victory. Out with every shilling you can spare to help to pass our target of

£300,000

SPACE DONATED BY

Flex Fasteners Ltd.
DINAS
Rhondda

Rhondda Salute the Soldier Natinal Savings campaign was held durin the week April 22nd-29th 1944. The target was £300,000. This target would maintain a Welsh battalion and medical unit for twelve months. Local firms paid for the adverts in the press. The final total was £414,818. The American Army played a role in the activities. The troops took part in the many parades and social events. There was a competition to guess the final total and the prize was won by an American G.I., W. Peckner.

CHAPTER 5

The Rhondda as a Training Ground

Towards the end of February 1944 the news was released to the local press that the American forces would arrive very shortly. The Rhondda Leader carried this information in its Editorial feature.

Saturday March 4th Editorial
Our Allies. Pontypridd and Rhondda people are famous for their hospitality. They have a chance during the next few weeks or more to show that famous hospitality because our Allies are coming. We have been expecting them for a month or so and a Committee representative of the United Churches and other local bodies is functioning in most of our Rhondda villages and preparing a proper reception for them. More important still the committees are preparing ways and means of helping Allied troops to pass their spare time pleasantly and profitably while they are among us.

The Rev. M.S. Hopkins and his joint committee for Porth and district have for weeks been preparing entertainment and other diversions for the lads. There was speculation that they might be arriving straight from the United States and landing at the South Wales ports.

This had been the case with the 28th Infantry Division which had debarked at ports in South Wales. (An American infantry division consisted of 15,000 to 20,000 men.) This Division was the Pennsylvanian National Guard whose shoulder flash was in the shape of a red keystone the seal of the Pennsylvanian State. They arrived on October 18th 1943 and spent six months training in South Wales before moving on to Chiseldon in Wiltshire.

They were replaced by the 2nd Infantry Division whose easily recognisable Indianhead shoulder flash became a common sight in Glamorgan particularly in Bridgend where many thousands were stationed at Island Farm Camp and under canvas in the surrounding fields. Their Headquarters was at St. Donats Castle. As the buildup continued they were joined in South Wales by the 90th and 75th Infantry Divisions.

These were not the troops destined to be billeted in the Rhondda but soldiers from these Infantry Divisions ventured into the Rhondda area on training exercises. One company camped on Dinas Isaf Farm in Trebanog in appalling weather. Days of continuous rain had turned the campsite into a mudbath. Muriel Thomas and Janet Rawlings can remember these young G.I.s congregating outside the Black Diamond Hotel looking soaking wet, cold, fed up and far from home. They were sleeping in tiny pup tents in these atrocious conditions. They were invited into local people's homes to get some comfort and experience some Rhondda hospitality.

Another batch of infantry soldiers set up camp on land belonging to Gelli-Fron Farm now occupied today by the scrapyard below Penrhiwfer Infants School. They used waste ground by the House of Trees as a firing range for rifle grenades and practising with demolition charges. They put notices up promising a concert by members of their company to be performed in the local Working Men's Club. However there was a tremendous rainstorm and the whole camp was flooded out and the site had to be abandoned. The good folk of Penrhiwfer never got their concert.

The same picture was repeated in various parts of the Rhondda during March and April 1944. Tented encampments would appear remain for a few days then disappear. The Bwlch, Rhigos and Maerdy Mountains featured prominently in this military activity. Where were the American troops destined for the Rhondda at this time? Unknown to their future hosts they were in fact quite near. Far from being fresh troops from the States they had been in Britain since mid-1943.

One Battalion was in a camp at Malpas, Newport while another Battalion was split between Cardiff and Barry. All were working in the docks of the three ports.

One incursion by the American Army is well remembered by the older residents of Clydach Vale. Close to mid-night in early April 1944 the population of this small mining community witnessed an unusual sight. There were large numbers of fully armed troops making their way through the darkened streets in battle order, that is, moving spaced out and keeping close to the sides of the houses. Initially it caused some alarm, they had been spotted by people doing fire-watching duties, who spread the news. When it was realised these were American soldiers the alarm turned to excitement and everyone turned out to witness this remarkable event.

There was a beautiful "bombers moon" so despite the Blackout the night was like day. What was being viewed was a night march by the 28th Infantry Division on exercise. They had marched across the mountain from Pricetown in the Ogmore Valley to Clydach Vale, a distance of about six miles.

They moved down the main road then formed up into an organised column in the area of the Mid-Rhondda Workingmens Club, known locally as the "Monkey Club". One section crossed the road bridge over the railway incline and marched on down through Gilfach Road to Tonypandy. The remainder marched down Court Street to Pandy Square. Waiting for them in Tonypandy was a long line of huge American trucks which transported them to the forested grounds of Glyncornel House where they set up camp.

All this military activity, with the novelty of them being Americans, caused an almost carnival atmosphere with hundreds out watching. With the words "Got any Gum, Chum", the children from the Terraces were besieging the camp at first light.

THE AMERICAN ARMY ARRIVES IN MID-RHONDDA
Remembered by Bryan Morse

I awoke with a start, it was night and pitch dark. As an eight-year-old boy in wartime, it was nothing new to wake to some alarm or another. Usually it was the air-raid siren and once when bombs dropped on Glyncornel House. When the siren went we would go down to the cwtch under the stairs.

There was a strange noise outside in the street. I entered my parents' bedroom and found them looking anxiously down into the street below. It seemed like a river of shapes.

Down the stairs we went and cautiously opened the door and what an amazing sight. There were no street lamps but moonlight and the light from a few opened doors illuminated the scene. Neighbours wearing coats over their nightwear talked excitedly and the noise revealed itself. A long column of soldiers wearing round helmets were marching down Gilfach Road, a few of them had hand held torches.

A window shot down above us and Mrs. Smith called down, "Is it the Germans Mr. Phillips?" The air raid warden shouted up, "It's all right, Mrs. Smith, it's the Americans, it's the Yanks."

Some of the neighbours shouted greetings. Some one in this moving mass shouted back with a rich American accent. In a matter of minutes, they were gone. The noise flowed slowly downhill, got quieter and quieter, and then ceased.
It was back to bed for everyone, I couldn't wait for the morning.

Next morning I heard the news, "The Americans are up on Dewinton Field." The soldiers had set up camp in Glyncornel Woods and all their trucks and jeeps were parked on Dewinton Field.

This news sent me and a friend hurrying up to Pandy Square. Access to the field was closed by a barrier manned by police and American servicemen. However, entry was gained via a side lane of St Andrews Church.

It was an exciting scene. There were a large number of American trucks, a few tents and everywhere activity and noise. Many of the trucks had their engines running and there were soldiers everywhere.

We ran on to the field and my friend shouted up to one of the trucks, "Got any Gum , Chum" and raced on. A voice shouted "Hey Kid, hang on" and the door of the truck swung open. Invited to climb up I mounted the metal steps and looked into the huge cab.

A khaki clad figure with his back to me was rummaging behind the canvas seats. He turned holding a handful of sweets and with a broad smile handed them to me. I was amazed, he was a black American soldier, he was the first black man I had ever seen.

He escorted me safely off the field and I ran home clutching my sweets, pausing only by Farmers Stores to see what I had been given.

The black American truck drivers who became such a common sight on the Rhondda roads were members of the 89th Quartermaster Mobile Battalion of the Transportation Corps.

THE ARRIVAL OF AMERICAN TROOPS IN MID-RHONDDA, APRIL 1944
Remembered by Gwyn Evans

A week before Easter 1944, a Sunday night, together with my mother and aunt, I had been visiting their sister, my aunt, living at High Street, Clydach Vale.

At 11.30 p.m. we set out to walk home to Tonypandy. In the absence of traffic we took to the centre of the road for our journey. That night there was a full moon of such brilliance that rooftops and roadway were glittering ribbons of silver light, enhanced by the wartime blackout.

As we approached the Central Hotel, Blaenclydach, we were conscious of a strange swishing sound that grew louder and filled the air around us. Being curious as to its source we turned to look back along the length of Clydach Road we had just walked. What we saw filled us with fear. On each side of the street, in deep shadow, as far as the eye could see, were lines of hunched figures, helmets glinting dully in the moonlight. Our immediate thoughts were that German paratroops had landed, so in self preservation we ran to hide down the side street opposite the Central Hotel, pressing ourselves against a wall.

The leading men of the columns passed by when a single figure broke free and made towards us. Imagine our relief when we recognised him as an American. At this point in time the helmets were not unlike those of the Germans when seen at night. The lone figure proved to be an officer who soon put us at our ease. It seemed that his unit had just made a night march across the mountain from somewhere in the region of Pricetown in the Ogwr Valley and were to rendezvous with the rest of the company at Tonypandy Square.

He accompanied us for the rest of the way to Tonypandy and on arriving at the Square we found it bustling with men and vehicles.

Many of the American troops were under canvas in Glyncornel Woods, they recruited the young boys of the area to run errands to the shops in Tonypandy. One incentive apart from the inevitable gum, was the large tips they gave to the boys. Sometimes in the region of 2/- (two shillings) or 2/6 (half a crown). In 1944 for this sum one could buy a three course meal. My reward was a joystick cigarette which I took for my aunt.

I lost further contact with the Americans during their stay as at the end of Easter Week 1944 I was admitted to Tyntyla Isolation Hospital for four weeks stay, with scarlet fever.

These American troops camped in Glyncornel Woods and who trained on the mountains above Llwynypia were part of the ill-fated 28th Infantry Division, who in the Campaign in Europe were to suffer the heaviest losses of any American Division. They joined the battle for Normandy on July 22nd 1944 assembling north of St. Lo. Here the 28th Infantry Division pushed into the struggle in the hedgerow country, the Bocage.

After heavy fighting the Division left the hedgerows behind and advanced over open country to the Seine.

On the 29th of August the 28th marched through the thronging streets and under the Arc de Triomphe, part of the victory parade through Paris in the celebration of the capture of the city. The men were not allowed to remain in Paris they moved east without pause into combat again. They moved into Belgium and finally after a great deal of fighting they reached the German Border.

In November 1944, the Division under inept commanders, was ordered to attack the Germans in the Hurtgen Forest near the Siegfried Line. Resistance was fierce and they suffered seventy-five percent casualties. It resulted in the destruction of an entire American Division with a total of 26,000 killed or injured.

The battered remnants were moved to a quiet area in the Ardennes. This "quiet" area by a cruel twist of fate lay right in the path of the German Ardennes Offensive, "The Battle of the Bulge", and what was left of the 28th Division was in the thick of the fighting once again.

Source:- ("Follow Me and Die", The Destruction of an American Division in World War 2. by Cecil B. Currey)

CHAPTER 6

The Arrival

The Americans are coming. During April, Rhondda residents had seen an increasing American presence. They had been much in evidence during Salute the Soldier Week. Those who by reason of their work had to travel out of the Rhondda were aware of camps springing up and an increasing number of American jeeps and trucks on the roads. Like an incoming tide the American Army was encroaching inland away from the coast where they had been based for some time. Units of the 28th Infantry Division had been in Porthcawl since the beginning of 1944. By the end of April there were over 70,000 U.S. troops in South Wales with over 40,000 in Glamorgan. There were large numbers in Newport, Cardiff and Barry already but now places like Cowbridge, Bridgend and Llantrissant saw camps setting up around them.

Black American troops were seen for the first time. The majority were units linked to the S.O.S (Services of Supply) and were members of the Transportatation Corps or U.S.Engineer Battalions.

Advance parties of U.S.troops were already in the Rhondda during the month of April billeted in hotels or buildings requisitioned by the Military Authorities such as Porth House in Porth.

It was during May that the great influx of American soldiers was to arrive here. Secrecy was paramount. Any information was on a need to know basis. All civil officials had taken an oath of secrecy. Communications were by courier, mail could be mislaid or lost. Any written communication was stamped Secret.

All was ready. The feeding stations had been built and equipped. The food stores were well stocked.

Billeting lists were stacked in the local police stations under lock and key. The Town Clerk and his officials were awaiting a telephone call. Among all those concerned, there was a growing feeling of excitement and anticipation. Months of planning were about to come to fruition.

The call came. They were on their way.

In the mining town of Trehafod the pumping engines, winding gear and the shunting of coal trucks was a constant background noise.

However, this was a different sound and coming from the direction of Pontypridd, a steady drone growing more audible every minute. Curious surface workers moved to the colliery gate entrance and were joined by the families from the houses opposite who came out onto their doorsteps.

It was the residents of Bryn Eirw, a terrace of houses higher up on the mountainside who first saw the source of the noise. Between the gaps in the houses below lorries could be seen.

Around the bend of Coed Cae Road, a jeep appeared bearing a red flag followed closely by a convoy of army trucks. Each huge olive-green truck bore a white five-pointed star and was laden with petrol cans, ropes, canvas bags and a deep treaded spare wheel. Most of the trucks were carrying troops. The convoy over a hundred strong was interspersed with a few squat weapons carriers and Dodge ambulances. It moved on to Porth and assembled on Llwyncelyn field. This was the first of several convoys that day.

So it was on the 14th of May 1944 that the main body of American troops arrived in the Lower Rhondda to join those already here who had been working as advance parties preparing for their arrival. These Americans were members of the 517 Port Battalion of the Transportation Corps.

The 517 Port Battalion, commanded by Lieut-Colonel Harold E. Bonar, was made up of four companies numbering 21 officers and 949 enlisted men. The 797th and 798th Port Companies were billeted in and around Porth. The 799th Port Company was billeted in Penygraig and the 800th Port Company in Ferndale.

In the Rhondda Fawr the larger of the two valleys workers on the early shifts were puzzled by the non-arrival of their buses. Police stood at strategic points and controlled what early morning commercial traffic was about. On the crowded railway platforms passengers wondered at the delay.

All was soon to be revealed. Heading up the valley roads came convoys of American trucks some carrying troops others supplies. Rail travellers were amazed to see the arrival of trains loaded with U.S. troops. At each station from Tonypandy to Treherbert hundreds of soldiers disembarked loaded with kitbags and carrying weapons.

The 487 Port Battalion was arriving. It was commanded by Lieut. Colonel Montgomery C. Jackson and was composed of the 184th, 185th, 186th and 187th Port Companies with the 282nd and 283rd Port Companies added to 517th Port Battalion on April 1st 1944. The total complement was 33 officers and 1,406 enlisted men.

The mass arrival of the American troops resulted in a great deal of activity. The billeting of them in private homes was a feat in itself. Local police officers supervised the arrangements and everything went smoothly.

This friendly invasion caused a great deal of excitement. Every move the troops made was watched by curious and enthusiastic crowds.

Within days, everything was running smoothly thanks to the planning of the civil and military authorities.

The Thistle Hotel in Tonypandy served-as the Headquarters for the 487 Port Battalion, officers from the Battalion were billeted there. The photograph shows two American sentries guarding the premises with an American Army truck parked opposite. Enlisted men were billeted in the Llwynypia Social and Non-Political Club next door to the Thistle Hotel. This building visible in the photograph was known locally as the "Greasy Waistcoat".

*The old Town Hall (a former theatre) was the main food store
for the U.S. Army billeted in the Rhondda area.*

Why were the 487 and 517 Port Battalions moved into the Rhondda?

They were basically dock workers, stevedores trained for the efficient loading and unloading of ships.

The 517 Port Battalion had been employed in Cardiff and Barry Docks since September 1943. The 487 Port Battalion had landed in Britain on September 4th 1943 and had worked at Newport Docks from January 5th 1944.

In the early months of 1944, there came a significant and dangerous change in the role they were to play in the forthcoming invasion. Companies from both Battalions were sent to the Assault Training Centres at Slapton Sands in Devon and at Mumbles near Swansea for training in amphibious operations.

Both Battalions were then attached to the First United States Army for operations with Engineer Special Brigades. The 487 Port Battalion was attached to the 5th Special Engineer Brigade and the 517 Port Battalion to 6th Special Engineer Brigade.

The combat engineers had the most complex job. Almost one quarter of U.S. troops going in on D-Day would be combat engineers. Their tasks more or less in order were to demolish beach obstacles, blow up mines on the beach and erect signs guiding incoming landing craft through cleared channels set up in panels to bring in troops and equipment.

To increase their combat readiness the American troops embarked on training exercises on the Rhondda mountains. They trained for the six weekdays and had Sunday off as a rest day. In the evenings they would sample the delights the Rhondda had to offer. There were many cinemas, pubs and dancehalls. Many just enjoyed the homely atmosphere their billets offered, a chance to live a normal life as they would at home. A G.I. Pfc Arthur Bonner wrote home, "People were so kind and willing. They gave us the key and let us do as they would have their own sons do."

This became a common sight on the Rhondda streets. These are troops from the 487 Port Battalion.

CHAPTER 7

The American Battalions: A Background

THE 517 PORT BATTALION TRANSPORTATION CORPS

The 517 Port Battalion was billeted in private homes in the towns throughout the Rhondda Fach with Porth serving as the administrative centre. One Company was billeted in the Penygraig area.

The Battalion was activated on February 16th at Seamills Camp Bristol under the command of Major N. Cerefice. It comprised of approximately 1,000 men split into four companies with a Headquarters and Headquarters Detachment. Their duties were the discharging the cargo from ships at Avonmouth Docks.

By September 1943 the Battalion had moved to Hayes Lane Camp at Barry. Three Companies worked at Barry Docks and one moved to Cardiff Docks. Their duties were the discharging of cargo from ships at these docks.

Then came a significant and dangerous change in the role they were to carry out. On the l9th of February the command of C Company was taken over by Captain Philo V. Dunbar and eight days later the Company moved from Barry to the Transportation Corps Training School at Mumbles, Swansea, for training in amphibious operations with the 1st and 5th Engineer Special Brigades. Training was completed on the 12th of March after two amphibious exercises and the Company returned to Barry on that date.

On the 13th of March 1944 B Company moved to Torquay for amphibious training on nearby Slapton Sands with the 6th Engineer Special Brigade. On the 10th of April B Company completed its training and returned on that date.

On these amphibious exercises Companies B and C had been training in the use of "Ducks". Duck amphibious trucks were widely used on D-Day: each could carry about 50 men or the equivalent weight in stores, from landing ships and across the beaches. They were aptly nicknamed from its technical designation DUKW (D: 1942 year of design; U: utility,

K: all wheel drive, W: dual rear axles). The 36 foot long Duck had a top speed of about 5 knots at sea and 50 mph on land.

On the 7th of April 1944 Major Donald N. Cerefice was relieved of command of the Battalion. He was transferred to be Commanding Officer of the 490th Port Battalion, a black American unit. On that same date Lt.Col. Harold E. Bonar assumed command of the 517 Port Battalion per Special Order 83, Headquarters Western Base Section dated 31st March 1944. Lt.Col. Bonar had served as an Infantry Officer in the First World War.

On April 29th 1944 the organisation of the Battalion was redesignated.

OLD DESIGNATION	NEW DESIGNATION
517th Hq. & Hq. Det. Port Bn. TC	517th Hq.&Hq.Det.Port Bn.TC
A Company	797 Port Company
B Company	798 Port Company
C Company	799 Port Company
D Company	800 Port Company

During this period there was constant talk of invasion, not alone by the military, but newspapers, radios, people in the street, the air war was being stepped up, and the American 8th Air Force was hammering the Pas de Calais area nearly every day. With two of the companies undergoing amphibious training there was a growing awareness that the 517 Port Battalion was to take part in the Invasion of Europe. It was on the 10th of April that the Battalion received notification that it was alerted and was attached to the First United States Army for operations with Engineer Special Brigades.

In early May the Battalion moved into the Rhondda Valleys, their work in the docks had been superceded by the need to prepare for their new role.

Troops of the 517 Port Battalion U.S. Army form up after a training exercise. This photograph was taken of the 799th Port Company billeted in Penygraig. It is possibly near the area of rough grassland lying below the House of Trees in Penrhiwfer where there was an American firing range. It was a common sight to see these soldiers marching up to this range.

THE 487 PORT BATTALION TRANSPORTATION CORPS

The 487 Port Battalion was formed on Nov 30th 1942 at Indiantown Gap Military Reservation in Pennsylvania when four companies i.e. 184th, 185th, 186th 187th Port Companies then known as companies A, B, C and D were activated and began to function and train under the Headquarters bringing them into being. Their Commanding Officer was Lt. Colonel M.C. Jackson.

Consisting of approximately 1,000 men split into the four companies it had men from almost every State in the Union including Hawaii. In April 1943 the Battalion moved to Fort Hamilton in New York then on to Camp Patrick Henry, Virginia on August l0th. Ten days later the Battalion set sail from Newport News, Virginia for Britain arriving in Glasgow in Scotland on the 24th of September 1943.

They were transported by train to Shirehampton near Avonmouth where they stayed for a month before moving again by train to Plymouth on October 6th 1943. They were the first U.S. troops in Plymouth. On

January 5th 1944 they went by train to a camp at Malpas, Newport South Wales. They were assigned to duties discharging cargo at Newport Docks.

They were assigned to a new role for the coming invasion of Europe. In April various companies underwent amphibious training at the Transportation Training School at Mumbles, Swansea and at Croyde Bay in north Devon.

In May they were moved by train to the Rhondda to await the call for the impending invasion. While here they were to improve their combat readiness by training on the mountains which enclose the Rhondda Valleys. A large number of American Army trucks arrived to transport them about and were a familiar sight on the Rhondda roads.

The 487 Port Battalion was billeted in private homes in the Rhondda Fawr, in Tonypandy, Llwynypia,Gelli, Ystrad, Ton Pentre,Treorchy and Treherbert.

The 487 and 517 Port Battalion were attached to the United States First Army on April 10th 1944 for operations with Engineer Special Brigades.

SERVICES OF SUPPLY

By March 1944 there were almost 150,000 black Americans in Britain. Most of them were in the Services of Supply mainly working in the ports unloading ships or driving trucks. The remainder were in Ordnance units and Engineering Companies. Black troops made up 60% of all Engineering Companies.

Detachments of black American troops were billeted in small groups in the Rhondda area. Members of the 89th Quartermaster Battalion had their headquarters in Maindy Barracks in Cardiff and a detachment billeted in the Drill Hall, the Territorial Barracks in Pontypridd. Their G.M.C. trucks with their black drivers were a common sight on the Rhondda roads. Further black supply troops were billeted in Bethany Chapel in Pwllgwaun and Soar Chapel in Hopkinstown.

Bill Keogh, Secretary of Bethany Chapel, records the presence of the American troops solved a financial problem. The money received from the American Authorities paid off the Chapel's debt. He recalls that some of the soldiers attended the chapel services. They were billeted in the basement. Soar Chapel is now demolished.

The Lucania and the Church Hall in Zion Street, Pontypridd, also housed black Americans. So pleased were they with the pleasant reception they had received while in Pontypridd that they provided a superb free concert featuring a danceband made up entirely of black musicians.

Some moved out prior to D-Day, all this group were gone by August 1st 1944. They were part of the vast system of organisation that unloaded and carried the millions of tons of supplies needed to support the Allied advance across Europe.

The 89th Quartermaster Battalion deserved special mention as they formed part of the Red Ball Express. So desperate were the shortages of ammunition, petrol and military supplies for the front line troops hundreds of miles inland from the ports in Normandy that Red Ball Highways were set up. The Services of Supply installed systems of transport by taking over main road routes in France and using most of these for one-way traffic. Along these Highways trucks were kept running continuously. Every vehicle ran at least twenty hours a day. Relief drivers were scraped up from every unit that could provide them and the trucks allowed to halt only for the necessary loading, unloading and maintenance. The trucks were given priority over all other traffic and had a red ball disc on their front.

The Commanding Officer, Lt-Col Joseph Fleischer and officers of the 89th Mobile Quartemaster Battalion

Senior N.C.O.s of the 89th Mobile Quartermaster Battalion

THE 89ᵗʰ QUARTERMASTER BATTALION (MOBILE) TRANSPORTATION CORPS

They had their Battalion Headquarters at Maindy Barracks in Cardiff from May 17ᵗʰ 1944. They were an important unit of the Services of Supply and were a trucking regiment. They used the general·purpose G.M.C. trucks and operated over a large area of South Wales.

Their Commanding Officer was Lt.-Col. Joseph Fleischer who was also Commanding Officer of all U.S. troops in the Cardiff area. Many thousands of American G.I.s were camped in every available open space including the Heath and Whitchurch areas and along the Penarth Road.

With the exception of sixteen white officers the 89ᵗʰ was an all American Negro unit. The black truck drivers were a familiar sight in the Rhondda Valleys where they were employed in the movement of troops and supplies.

Black soldiers in the Snow

This unusual photograph taken in a snowstorm shows a group of black American soldiers silhouetted against the snowy background in Gelli-wasted Road, Pontypridd. The lady on the right appears to be carrying a tray of warm drinks for them.

The bulk of the American Divisions in the eastern half of South Wales were elements of the Vll Corps commanded by Major General J. Lawton Collins and were to land on Utah Beach on D-Day. The Vll Corps were to battle across Europe from Normandy to the Elbe crossing the Rhine over the famous Remagen Bridge.

AMERICAN RAILWAY AUTOMOTIVES STORED AT PONTYPRIDD

Over a hundred American Army locomotives were stored on the line running from Tonteg to the Graig in Pontypridd prior to the D-Day Invasion. They were intended to be used on the captured French rail network and to replace French rolling stock destroyed by Allied air attacks.

Several black Transportation Corps Companies were billeted in the Pontypridd and lower Rhondda areas to carry out maintenance and drive these locomotives.

Two photographs show locomotives on this Pontypridd line, the third shows one of these locomotives being used to transport the 487 Port Battalion from Lison in France to Antwerp in Belgium in November, 1944.

26th INFANTRY DIVISION (YANKEE DIVISION)

In late March 1944 units of the 26th Infantry Division commanded by Maj. General Gerald Willard S. Paul were based in Trehafod and Hopkinstown in the lower Rhondda Valley and in Pontypridd. Officers from the Division were billeted in Porth House, Porth, and Pontypridd.

The 500th Parachute Infantry Regiment was attached to the 26th Infantry Division and Company B was billeted in Zion Chapel and St. Davids Church Hall in Hopkinstown These halls were for accommodation only. The Company numbered some 250 men. Conditions were very basic with the soldiers sleeping on the floor or on camp beds that could be folded or stored. The 509th was the oldest Parachute Regiment in the United States Army.

The 26th Infantry Division was one of the few American units to have experienced battle conditions. They had taken part in "Operation Torch", the invasion of North Africa and in the battle for Sicily in 1943. Now they were back in Britain preparing for the invasion of Europe.

These combat infantry troops were away training during the day on the surrounding mountains or practising with their weapons on the firing range near Treforest. They returned in the evening to their billets.

Pfc. Elmore O. Hartman
Pfc. Hartman from Harrisburg, Virginia, was a member of the 509th Parachute Infantry Regiment attached to the 26th Infantry Division. They were billeted in Hopkinstown from March to the end of May 1944.
He and his regiment campaigned through North Africa, Sicily, Normandy, Northern France, the Ardennes and the Rhineland. He was photographed aged 19 in Luxembourg. He was wounded in the fighting for Metz in March 1945.

Barbàra Davies recalls the period when these Americans were here as a time full of fun since the young soldiers joined in the social life of the area. She lived at that time in Trehafod and as a 17 year-old was employed as an assistant in Page Gowns in Pontypridd.

Page Gowns employed eight young female assistants and they together with other teenage girls flocked to the Park Ballroom where dances were held every weekend. The novelty of meeting these young American boys was a great attraction.

The Drill Hall off the Broadway acted as a transit camp for a variety of American units. It was a Territorial Army Barracks and housed in turn both white and black G.I.s, Rangers and American Army Nurses. The Americans had a PX Store in a building opposite the present day Boots Store. It was in an upstairs room and there was a constant stream of soldiers visiting there to obtain cigarettes, sweets, canned goods and other luxuries denied the ordinary citizen.

Barbara Davies in 1944

Parked on this grass verge are American jeeps and different types of G.M.C. Trucks.

This photograph shows troops from the 484 Port Battalion. It became a common sight in the Rhondda to see American G.I.s being transported in this manner.

*High Street, Pontypridd viewed from the back of an American Army truck in May 1944.
The truck was belonging to the 487 Port Battalion.*

A 487 Port Battalion Jeep

Four G.I.s billeted in Treherbert pictured by a Weapons Carrier

MEMORIES OF 1944

"There was a long convoy of large American trucks full of troops moving slowly through Penygraig. All the drivers were black soldiers." Edna Cochlin

"Although they had their breakfast in the cookhouse in Llanfair Church Hall in Penygraig my mother insisted that our G.I. guest would not leave her house hungry. So he had two breakfasts. " Betty Thomas

"There was a special invitation dance held for the Americans in Judges Hall in Trealaw. The G.I. staying with us asked my parents if I could go to keep him company. I was allowed to go and it was a marvellous night. I was in seventh heaven..." Jill Walters

"We had two G.I.s staying with us in Mikado Street in Penygraig. They had the run of the house. They took us all to the cinema which they called the movies." Peggy Gay

"I liked to watch the American soldiers playing baseball on Penrhiwfer playing fields." Megan Jones

"In 1944 I was living in Railway Terrace, Williamstown. Every night when the air-raid siren sounded we used to go down to the cwtch – under the stairs. I was working in Currans in Cardiff and getting up all the time in the night meant you were shattered going to work in the morning. My brother and I told my mother not to wake us that night if the siren sounded.

My mother was so worried about the air raids that she would get up from bed and sit at the bottom of the stairs. This particular night she shouted up the stairs "Ivor! What sort of helmets have the Germans got?" "Round," he answered. "The Germans are here," she said, "They are out the front sitting on the steps."

+We rushed to the window and looked down into the street. There were a large number of soldiers wearing round helmets. It was the Americans." Gwyneth Lockyer

"When the Americans marched up the mountain in Tonypandy we children followed them. They were throwing hand grenades into the second quarry by Pugh's Farm. We thought that was great." Don Lewis

"I was in the Army Cadets and together with the Home Guard we were on an exercise against the local American detachment. It had been a very hot day and it was getting dark. The exercise was being held on the mountains above Trehafod. I watched this American soldier struggle up the steep mountainside towards where I was hidden. I could hear him muttering to himself as he came near. As he passed within three feet of me I fired the blank in my Canadian Ross rifle. It sounded like a cannon and I really startled him and he tumbled down the slope. He used an awful lot of bad language." Gerwyn Rees

CHAPTER 8

The American Army in Porth and the Rhondda Fach

A large contingent of American troops were based in Porth and the lower Rhondda Fach as far as Ferndale. They were all members of the 517 Port Battalion. Preparations for their arrival had involved a great deal of activity which had begun early in 1944. The local newspaper records what happened.

Rhondda Leader February 26th 1944
Porth and District Reception Committee. At the meeting the Rev. D.J. Morgan (Hon. Sec.) emphasised the need for a canteen to be ready for immediate use should Allied troops arrive and they should make enquiries for a suitable premises. Members of the Committee are Mr. John Gwyn, Mr. E.T. Lloyd and the Rev. W.S. Evans (Treasurer).
The subcommittee consisted of the Rev. P.H. Fisher, Rev. F.S. Copleston and Messrs. A. Williams, Lloyd J. Davies and Stanley Williams. The Committee held a further meeting in Salem Chapel on March 1st.

The U.S. troops received a formal welcome at Tabernacle Chapel in Hannah Street, Porth and enjoyed an evening of musical items and community singing. Joan Thomas who as a young girl attended the concert remembers the chapel was packed, with people standing in the aisles

The G.I.s were billeted in private homes in Porth, the majority in the Llwyncelyn area. An encampment was set up in Llwyncelyn field now a factory site and base for the Porth Fire Brigade. Several huts and tents were set up to contain stores. A stockade was built and manned by U.S. Military Police. Prisoners were held there awaiting trial by a military court.

Two Nissen Huts had been constructed to serve as cookhouses. One was lower down the slope from the Old Tin Chapel that was the vestry for Porth Chapel. The Tin Chapel equipped with trestle tables served as a feeding station. The other Nissen Hut was erected next to the Rink Dancehall which doubled as a feeding station.

A regular morning sight was the daily ritual of the early morning march to the feeding stations where the G.I.s had their breakfast and morning roll call.

Joan Thomas recalls this taking place in Llwyncelyn, Porth. "They would gather at the corner of Gethin Terrace then march carrying their mess tins down to the Old Tin Chapel for breakfast. They sometimes would sing a marching song to keep in step. I used to watch them from my bedroom window. It was most unusual."

Porth House was for many years a T.B. Clinic. It was requisitioned in 1940 by the Military Authorities and in 1944 was used as the Headquarters for the 517 Port Battalion and housed the Headquarters Detachment. After the Battalion moved out on June 1ˢᵗ 1944 for the Normandy Invasion it continued to be used by the American Authorities to house officers from units based in and around the Pontypridd area.

A welcoming reception was held in Tabernacle Chapel in Porth for the American troops of the 517 Port Battalion. It was organised by the Porth and District Reception Committee made up of the Rev. D.J. Morgan (Hon. Secretary) Rev. W.S. Evans (Treasurer), John Cyyn, E.J. Floyd, Rev. P.H. Fisher, A. Williams, Rev. F.S. Copleston, Lloyd J. Davies and Stanley Williams.

Captain Maynard A. Steinberg was Adjutant to Lt. Colonel Harold E. Bonar Commander of the 517 Port Battalion. He held this position during the Normandy Campaign and later during their operations in the Port of Antwerp. During the time the Battalion was in the Rhondda he was part of the Headquarters Detachment based at Porth House, in Porth. Officers from this Detachment were billeted in Porth House and in the New York Hotel. Porth House was managed by Mrs. E. Powell who after the Normandy Invasion received many letters from officers formerly billeted there, some of which were printed in the Rhondda Leader.

61

A food store occupied the present day Porth Library and large amounts of canned products kept there under armed guard. A U.S. Army medical centre was set up in the basement of the New York Hotel and a Medical Detachment stationed there.

Senior U.S. Army officers were billeted in Porth House which had been requisitioned by the Government and managed by Mrs. E. Powell. Porth House is now the site of the Alec Jones Day Centre. Officers from the 26th Infantry Division were housed there. The building also served as Headquarters for the 517 Port Battalion.

Mrs. Powell received several letters from officers billeted there after their departure for Normandy, one of which was published in the Rhondda Leader of August 12th 1944.

News from Normandy. Mrs. E. Powell, Porth House, has recently received a letter from France written by Captain Howerd E. Newbern U.S.A. Forces recently stationed in Porth and Pontypridd district. Friends will be pleased to know that all is well with the Battalion. To quote from the letter, "Things are going along fine over here. Our boys are doing a really superior job of work. I am very proud indeed to be one of them." In sending his good wishes Captain Newbern said he will always remember Porth and Pontypridd where he made a great number of friends and sends his good wishes to all.

It is interesting to know that Mrs. Powell has also received a communication from Major J.L.Haefell U.S.A. Forces who was also at Pontypridd stating he is in France safe and well.

With hundreds of troops training in the area there was the problem of adequate showering facilities. The Council was approached on the matter.

Minutes of the Rhondda Council Health Committee Meeting May 23rd 1944. The Committee has received an application from the Officer in Charge of the Porth Detachment of U.S. troops for the use of showers at Porth swimming pool and this would be followed by similar applications in respect of other pools in the area when other detachments reached the district.

In effect Porth Pool had already been requisitioned and in use by the American forces and serving a wide area as far as Llantrisant. A large American tented camp had been set up on Llantrisant Common. To keep the showers constantly heated American soldiers were used to stoke the coal-fired boilers.

New York Hotel

The Medical Detachment of the 517 Port Battalion set up a Dispensary in the basement of the New York Hotel in Porth. It was commanded by Captain Santo F. Brancato M.D.

It was an ambulance and crew from this Dispensary that dealt with a serious incident on the Battalion's firing range in Treforest on May 24th 1944.

On the Treforest Range the 797th Port Company was firing carbines and Anti-tank grenades. During the course of the firing 3 grenades failed to detonate. These unexploded grenades were marked and when the company completed their days firing, two guards were posted on the range.

During the course of the evening the guards had occasion to drive away several groups of children who insisted on playing in the same area in which were the unexploded grenades. Later the guards heard an explosion and found three children injured and phoned the New York Dispensary.

Two of the children were taken by the ambulance to the Cottage Hospital in Pontypridd. The third boy had been fatally wounded and had died before the ambulance arrive

CONFIDENTIAL

HEADQUARTERS   /Ist
517th port bn Tc
APO I34 US Army

25 MAY I944

SUBJECT: Accident on Treforest Range.

To: Commanding Officer, xxIx District, APO 5I6 US Army.

I. On the 24 May I944 at Treforest, Range, Pontypridd, the 797th port Co of this battalion was firing carbines and AT grenades, M9aI.

2.During the course of the firing 3 grenades failed to detonate. These unexploded grenades were marked, and when the company completed their days firing, two guards were posted on the range.

3. The guards, pfc Edwin W. Arnold ASN I2005567, and Pvt. Raymond C. Sexton, ASN 34332759, stated that during the course of the evening they had occasion to drive away several groups of children who insisted on playing in the same area in which were the unexploded grenades.

4. The guards state that at approximately 2IIO hours they heard an explosion. They ran to the spot where the grenades were lying and they found three children injured from the explosion of the grenade. One guard went to summon an ambulance while the other applied first aid to the children.

5. An ambulance from 5I7[th] Port Bn dispensary arrived at the scene and took two of the children to the Cottage Hospital, Pontypridd. The third boy had been fatally wounded and died before the government ambulance arrived. The ambulance with the two injured boys arrived at the hospital at 2230 hours.

6.   The injured are:

   a.   Dennis Ritchens
        62 Tower St,Treforest, S. Wales
        Deceased. Public Mortuary, Pontypridd.

CONFIDENTIAL

Tunic Patches of American Units based in South Wales

Left: 28th. Division, departed for Normandy 24th July 1944.

Right: 2nd. Infantry Division, departed for Normandy June 7th 1944.

Left: 90th Infantry Division, departed for Normandy June 8th 1944.

Right: 75th. Infantry Division, departed for Europe at the end of 1944 and took part in the Battle of the Bulge.

Left: Europe Theatre of Operations. A star design in blue oval, lightning bolts in red splitting chain of yellow which indicates Advance Base.

Right: Army Amphibious Units. A blue patch with a curved top. The design consists of an anchor, an eagle and a submachine gun in yellow.

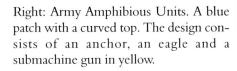

Left: Meritorious Service Insignia. Awarded to members of the 487 and 517 Port Battalions for the award of a Meritorious Unit Plaque for the part they played in the period 1st June 1944 to 1st August 1944

Right: Engineer Amphibian Command. A white oval with a blue inner border. In the centre is the figure of a sea horse in red.

Left and right: Unit badges of the transportation corps and services of supply

Unit Patch of the United States First Army

26th. Infantry Division "Yankee Division"

509th. Parachute Infantry Regiment

Unit Patch of the United States Third Army

Cap Patch. Airborne Forces

Unit Patch of the United States Medical Battalions

Greetings card sent to Pvt.. Lewis C. Shaw from his home town in Tampa, Florida.
Private Lewis was a member of the 497 Port Company, 517 Port Battalion, U.S Army

Wartime cards sent to Pvt. Lewis C. Shaw, U.S Army.
He was billeted with Mr William and Hilda Pearce at 50, Graigwen Road, Cymmer, Porth

The G.M.C. 2 1/2 truck. Over half a million were produced.
The "deuce and a half" was the workhorse of the American Army.
These American Army vehicles were a common sight in the Rhondda in 1944

The Dodge WC 54 Ambulance and Harley-Davidson motor cycle.
The 487 and 517 Port Battalion Medical Detachments had these ambulances. The 94th. Medical Battalion had them in large numbers.

Dodge Command Car. This is a WC 58 Radio Vehicle. The "S" suffix to its serial number indicates radio interference suppression equipment fitted

The Jeep. This 1/4 ton 4x4 truck was produced by Ford and Willys

Dodge Weapons Carrier. Dodge produced a quarter of a million T214 series 3/4 ton 4x4s

MERRY CHRISTMAS *and* HAPPY NEW-YEAR

☆ 487ᵗʰ PORT BATTALION T.C. ☆

1942
INDIANTOWN GAP
NEW YORK
ENGLAND
SOUTH WALES
NORMANDY
FRANCE
BELGIUM
1945?

The Battalion Christmas card sent by Pfc. Arthur Bonner to his parents in New Jersey for Christmas 1944. What would 1945 bring? Peace and a ticket home for Christmas 1945. The S.S. Argentina sailed from Le Havre, France on December 9th. 1945. The 487 Port Battalion was home.

Y Ddraig Goch flies proudly over farmland in Bulger, Pennsylvania, U.S.A.
It is the home of the former G.I. Pfc. Karl Gaber of the 186 Port Company,
487 Port Battalion, U.S. Army. A tangible link with the Rhondda of 1944.

b. Gerald Ramsell
23 Tower St Treforest, S. Wales.
Cottage Hospital Pontypridd

c. Kenneth Wilcox
112 Wood rd, Treforest, S Wales
Cottage Hospital, Pontyprid

7. Police Constable Hart of the Treforest Police was at the scene
shortly after the incident and received statements from witnesses.
Other persons who may have pertinent information are Dr. Arthur
Jenkins, Pontypridd, and John M. Hughes, 11 Cardiff Rd, Treforest.

8. The unit claims officer, Captain James J. Powell, Jr., 797th Port Co.
is investigating the case and will obtain statements from all
witnesses.

For the Commanding Officer

MAYNARD A. STEINBERG

CONFIDENTIAL

The 800th Port Company was billeted in Ferndale in private homes and
had their food in St. Dunstan's Church Hall, apparently damage was
caused to the hall floor by installing cooking stoves for which the church
received compensation. In his letter to Mrs. Murnane of Dyffryn Street
Sgt. Rocco Pardo was full of praise for the welcome given to his Company
by the people of Ferndale.

Not all of the troops went to the pubs and dancehalls, many took
advantage of the comforts of their adopted homes. By today's standards
there were few modern conveniences but the G.I.s enjoyed the
companionship of the local people.

As was the practice years ago on long summer evenings the residents would sit out in the street and talk. The windowsills provided seating and chairs were brought out from the house and placed on the pavements. Double summertime was in force during the war and it was light to almost midnight.

Muriel Williams from Ferndale recalls the American soldiers enjoyed these informal gatherings and many pleasant evenings were spent with them listening to their descriptions of home in the various parts of America. She remembers particularly two soldiers from the Bronx, a suburb of New York, marvelling at the starry skies, the Blackout of course adding to their beauty.

Endless pots of tea and coffee were brewed and the real American coffee was well appreciated. The seemingly endless supply of American cigarettes and cigars were enjoyed by the locals. The children had a great time sampling the gum and candy. The young girls thought it all very romantic.

The conversations would go on till the early hours. There was a homely friendly atmosphere and the young Americans enjoyed it immensely. Unfortunately D-Day was approaching and these pleasant evenings were to end too soon.

THE MILITARY POLICE STOCKADE

A temporary prison was constructed on the Llwyncelyn Field site in Porth. It was manned by members of the 793rd Military Police Battalion who had arrived in Pontypridd in February 1944. Units were based in Pontypridd, Porth and Caerphilly and then generally dispersed through the South Wales area under the control of Seventh Corps of the United States Army.

Black American troops were detained in the stockade. Prisoners were sent here from a wide area in South Wales. A former pool attendant recalls that they were brought up to Porth Baths in trucks accompanied by armed guards to use the showers. On occasions they were allowed in the pool but always closely supervised by armed American Military Police.

THE ITALIAN CONNECTION

A large number of the American soldiers billeted in the Rhondda were the sons and grandsons of Italian migrants to the United States. In 1944 there were Italian cafes in virtually every town and they proved natural meeting places for the G.I.s.

One such cafe was that owned by Serafino and Dorinda Bacchetta in Porth. Every evening it would be crowded with off-duty soldiers. It is still run by the Bacchetta family in the persons of the brothers Aldo and Ronato. In this picture they have taken a few minutes off from their busy cafe to pose with some mementos from 1944. Ronato holds a U.S. Army torch left behind in the sudden departure for Normandy whereas Aldo holds a table knife stamped U.S. Army. There was an acute shortage of cutlery at this time and a "Sgt. Bilko" from the local 798th Port Company did a spot of unofficial Lend Lease and solved the problem. Aldo holds one of the survivors.

"U.S. Servicemen were regular customers for coffee and sarsaparilla drinks. They would chat up the female customers and staff to arrange dates. It was easy for them, they were the ones with sweets, gum, cigarettes and silk stockings." Aldo Bacchetta

The cafe in 1944

Mr and Mrs Bacchetta

MEMORIES FROM 1944

"I was in the Home Guard and I was on my way to Pentre Barracks when I met two very smart American officers as they got off the train in Pentre. They asked me the whereabouts of the Thistle Hotel in Tonypandy. They had booked accommodation there. They were probably seeing to the arrangements for the troops that were to follow." Bill Lewis

"Because the Americans were here in Porth Hannah Street was packed with people in the evenings. When you went to the cinema it seemed to be full of soldiers smoking cigars. I loved the smell of cigars." Joan Thomas

"The American troops used to march up to Porth Baths wearing all their battle gear and carrying their weapons after they had been on exercises. I was fascinated with them." Gerwyn Rees

"When my mother was told that an American soldier was going to be billeted at our house in Treherbert she emptied the spare room of all the odds and ends. She decided because it looked so shabby she would decorate the room. She had a bucket of distemper mixed when there was a knock on the door. It was the American, when he saw what she was about to do he took the brush from her and distempered the room himself. He was a lovely person." Peggy Rose

"The Americans in Porth were very friendly and generous to the children. One group staying in Glyn Fach had a pet fox which we loved going to see. When they left in a long convoy I saw the fox travelling with them on a weapons carrier." Tal Williams

"We put on a small show for some American officers in Treherbert Boys School. We sang "Brother James's Air". I liked to watch them training on the mountain." Roy Jones

"The American soldiers used to march to Sunday Mass at the Catholic Church, St.Gabriels in Tonypandy. I say march but it was more of a casual amble with them talking among themselves." Geof. Drake

"I remember the Americans well because I met them daily at work. I was employed at Austins in Treforest assembling jeeps and all types of trucks. We worked under American military supervision.

I can recall sitting in the Turberville Arms in Penygraig and the bar being crowded with G.I.s. They were handing out cigars to everyone. I had never smoked a cigar before and these were the real thing. The room was full of cigar smoke as we all puffed away." Reg. Owen

"From my bedroom window in Ystrad I had a clear view of Nantgwyddon Road. There seemed to be an endless convoy of slow moving trucks. The American Army was leaving the Rhondda." Hywel Gillard

CHAPTER 9

The American Army in Mid-Rhondda

The American Army was much in evidence in the Mid-Rhondda area. Hundreds of troops from the 487 Port Battalion were billeted in houses in Tonypandy and Llwynypia. The majority housed in Gilfach Road, Primrose Street and Kenry Street were members of the 184th Port Company. Isolated groups were scattered about such as the platoon based in the New Inn at the top of Clydach Vale.

Again it was the same pattern followed throughout the Rhondda. The G.I.s slept in the houses but were fed at special feeding centres. In Tonypandy a Nissen Hut was erected on land adjacent to Zion Chapel to serve as a cookhouse. This area is now occupied by the Kwik-Save store. The Victoria Billiard Hall which lay to the rear of the long established Chemist Shop was used as a dining hall.

The old Town Hall was requisitioned for use as a general store and distribution centre for the American Army. It was a common sight to see the huge American G.M.C. and Dodge trucks loading and unloading tinned foodstuffs and all the various supplies needed to maintain the large number of troops in the area. It was apparently a popular place for local people to gather in the hope that something would literally fall of the back of a lorry. The G.I.s aware of all the shortages suffered by the people took a liberal approach as to what goods had been damaged in transit and could be regarded as unfit for storage and could therefore be given away. The Town Hall was a Mecca for the local children who would gather in a crowd confident that chocolate and chewing gum would come their way.

The Dewinton Field now occupied by Tonypandy Health Centre and the Council Yard was used by the Americans for the parking and maintenance of military vehicles and the whole area was under armed guard. The local troops assembled there every morning for roll call. Areas inside the walled Glamorgan Colliery Yard was also used for the storage of military equipment including amunition.

In the early evenings after mealtimes the pavements in the area of Pandy Square were crowded with American G.I.s deciding how to pass the evening away. They were spoilt for choice. There were three cinemas if they wanted to watch a movie as they termed it. There was the Picturedrome on their doorstep and further down the Empire Cinema now the site of the Woolworth store. At the bottom of the town was the Plaza Cinema.

If they decided to try the novelty of the local public houses for a pint and a singsong, every pub had a piano, there were plenty to chose from. There was the Pandy Inn, Dewinton Hotel, White Hart, Adare Hotel, Bridgend Hotel, Cross Keys and the Dunraven Hotel. The last three are now demolished. There were of course many clubs and the G.I.s were often taken there by their hosts. A fact recorded for posterity in a letter written by Pvt. Gilbert White to Mr. Gwyn Jones of 7 Primrose Street, Tonypandy with whom he was billeted:

Give my regards to all the boys in the club and hope you get down there at times. I know how you enjoy it. I have been in Cherbourg and had a few drinks of Calvados, but its pretty terrible stuff. It's pretty bad to beat your Welsh beer.

The letter is dated June 25th 1944, the German Garrison at Cherbourg surrendered the next day, the 26th, after much heavy fighting.

It is worth recording the drinking of alcoholic drinks was not the normal practice for the young Americans many of whom came from "dry" States but these were not normal times. Despite the lifting of Prohibition, states like Oklahoma remained dry.

Pat Davies's father Tom Davies was landlord of the White Hart in Tonypandy recalls these times clearly. It was very popular with the local American troops. She recalls the soldiers would arrive as a large jovial crowd and fill the pub. The regulars enjoyed the company of the G.I.s particularly since they seemed to have an abundance of cigarettes and sweets that were generously distributed. Overpaid by our standards they may have been and could not understand our money but were intent on parting with it. Our beer was not exactly to their taste and they would ask for bourbon or spirits that were in short supply. Some nights the beer would run out.

There were always shortages particularly of beer glasses and customers would bring their own or bring jam jars. The pub would be full of good-natured noise or if a pianist turned up there would be a general singsong.

All would be proceeding normally then the door would open and all fall quiet. Three American Military Police would enter wearing their white helmets and carrying big white night sticks. The sergeant in charge was a giant of a man and on his belt he carried a large holster containing a pistol. Pat recalls he would call out to her father "OK Boss no trouble here?" Receiving a favourable answer he would bid good night and continue on his rounds.

As soon as they left everything would continue as before. Pat commented "There never was any trouble they were a nice bunch of boys. We were sad when they left knowing what was facing them."

The Brigand Hotel in the 1940's
The stone pillar of the entrance leading to the wooden steps descending to the
air raid shelter can just be seen in the bottom right corner of the picture.

The Bridgend Hotel in Tonypandy was another popular pub with American servicemen. A large number of G.I.s were in camps in and around Bridgend. Many of them had struck up friendships with local girls who worked in the Arsenal in Bridgend and came up to spend weekends in the Rhondda.

Mr. and Mrs. Jack Davies were popular hosts and made the Americans welcome. After the Invasion many of them wrote letters and cards back to the Bridgend Hotel maintaining the friendly links. When the main influx of troops arrived in May 1944 the pub was packed to the door every night.

Gwen Elston at that time owned a hairdresser's shop next to the old Town Hall and remembers the Americans well. The Town Hall served as the main food store for all the units in the Rhondda. She often helped out as a barmaid in the Bridgend Hotel to help cope with the large number of American troops. On occasions, on beer delivery days, Mr. Jack Davies would end up somewhat inebriated together with his American friends in the pub cellars. Then an urgent request would come across to the hairdresser's shop for help.

She remembers some happy times there, the G.I.s were pleasant and good natured and out to enjoy themselves. They were billeted in private homes in Tonypandy and many came with their hosts to the pub to have a good time together. There were great sing-songs with both local people and Americans providing contributions of singing talent.

Gwen Elston had deferment from military service because her job was classified as a reserved occupation. However she still had to carry out a role of an Air Raid Warden. She was in charge of the local air raid shelter. This was a tunnel that ran under the main road and the Town Hall. Access to the shelter was by means of a wooden staircase which led down to the entrance. This was adjacent to a tunnel carrying the river under the road. It was a grim rat infested place and little used by local people. Its only popular use was as a courting spot for the local American G.I.s and their girlfriends. Double summer time was in force and it was light until 11pm.

Her duty had to be carried out and Gwen and her steel helmet, several sizes too large had to put in an appearance. She recalls "I hated the place, only the courting couples were there, I felt I was playing gooseberry."

When the day arrived for the Americans to depart for the Invasion of Normandy the troops assembled outside the Llwynypia Social and Non-Political Club, known locally as the "Greasy Waistcoat". This club had been used to billet some of the soldiers. The date was June 1st 1944. A convoy of American trucks were lined up waiting for the troops. When the news spread they were leaving a crowd gathered. Eventually they left to shouts and waves from the crowd. Some looking on were in tears.

Gwen Elston saw their departure and described it as a very moving experience. Life in Tonypandy returned to its normal pattern. She received many letters addressed simply to the "Lady Hairdresser, Tonypandy" and she distributed them to the named friends, male and female.

THE AMERICAN TREAT

A time recalled by Winnie Howells.

There were three American soldiers billeted with my mother at 139 Primrose Street, Tonypandy. Irwen Roberts and Louis Proto were from the Bronx in New York, the third soldier, a sergeant is a name I can't recall.

They were aware of all the wartime shortages and took every opportunity to bring us extra food as well as cigarettes and sweets. Some of the canned products particularly the fruit and meat products were real treats. So my parents were full of anticipation when Louis Proto appeared one afternoon carrying a large tin partly hidden under his jacket. He announced he wanted everyone to stay out of the kitchen while he prepared a real American meal.

My mother sent a message to our house, just several doors away, inviting myself and my husband Hermas to this feast. All the family sat around the table while Louis carried out his secret cooking operation in the kitchen.

At last he entered carrying a large tureen. We all looked up eagerly as with a flourish he removed the lid to reveal the real American meal – it was American sweet corn. He doled out a large helping on to each plate and then joined us for the feast. I hope the expression on our faces didn't betray what we really thought about the meal.

We struggled through the meal making the appropriate appreciative comment. The sweet corn was something we had not eaten before and it was not to our taste. We all agreed with Louis that the meal really was something special.

When we returned to our house, my husband commented that we fed that sort of stuff to chickens in this country.

Fortunately, Louis was unable to get hold of another tin of American sweet corn.

Pvt. Bill Rombercich was billeted with Mrs. Violet Lewis in Thomas Street, Tonypandy. He was a cook with the 184 Port Company, 487 Port Battalion. His son arrived in Britain with an Infantry Division as he left for France with his Battalion.

Ready for Chow

G.I.s from the 186 Port Company, 487 Port Battalion pictured outside their mess hall and cookhouse. The buildings are specially constructed Nissen Huts. This Company was billeted in Treherbert. Several of these huts were constructed in the Rhondda to serve as cookhouses for the American troops. There were two in Porth, one adjacent to Zion Chapel on Pandy Square, one to the rear of Pentre Legion and another in Taff Street in Treherbert next to the Band Hut. The type of hut took its name from Lt.-Col. P.N. Nissen (1871-1930) its designer.

The official welcome for the troops of the 487 Port Battalion billeted in Tonypandy and Llwynypia was held in Salem Chapel, Salem Terrace, Llwynypia. That chapel has now been demolished and replaced with a smaller modern chapel.

The reception was held on Monday evening on May 22nd 1944 and was fully reported in the local press.

Rhondda Leader May 27th 1944
Allies Welcomed. Ward 5 took a lead in welcoming Allied forces when a concert was held in their honour at Salem Chapel on Monday evening presided over by the Rev. D. Davies (Vicar of Clydach Vale).

Speeches of welcome were made by Councillor David Phillips (Chairman of the Rhondda District Council), Sidney Mitchell, W.S. Lane, D.J. Richards, Mr. D.J. Jones O.B.E. (Clerk of the Rhondda District Council), the Rev. Hayden Rees (Vicar of Llwynypia) and Teifionydd Hughes (Gosen) Blaenclydach and Colonel John Evans (Home Guard).

On behalf of the Allied Forces Chaplain Whiley and Colonel Jackson paid tribute to the reception and hospitality extended to them in the Rhondda.

A delightful musical programme arranged by Mr. Selwyn Hammond consisted of items by Misses Edith Hickman , Tonypandy and Joan Llewellyn, Pontypridd (Sopranos) and Mr. Edward Havard, Bedlinog (Baritone). Mr. Hammond himself rendered selections on the organ and accompanied the singers.

Much preparatory work for the occasion had been done by an enthusiastic committee of which Mr. E.A. Lewis is Chairman and Mr. B. Morgan is Secretary ably assisted by Councillor Sidney Mitchell and Mrs. Herbert Jones (Entertainment Secretary).

The reception for the soldiers of the 487 Port Battalion billetted in Tonypandy and Llwynypia was held at Salem Chapel, Llwynypia on Monday May 22nd 1944. It was attended by Lt. Col. Montgomery C. Jackson and officers and men from the Battalion.

Ellen Lewis is a lifelong member of Salem Chapel and remembers the reception vividly.

A large crowd assembled in the chapel. The front pews were empty, reserved for our American guests. The audience was treated to a first class concert.

After the meeting we mixed socially with the Americans. Many were invited to our homes and there were many parties in the weeks that followed.

One of the girls made it known that she had a bathroom in her house. This was a rarity in those days. She generously offered its facilities to our American guests. As a result her parents had the company of American soldiers virtually every evening who formed a small queue outside her home clutching their soap and towels.

(The old Salem Chapel was destroyed by fire in August 1986 and a new smaller chapel occupies the site.)

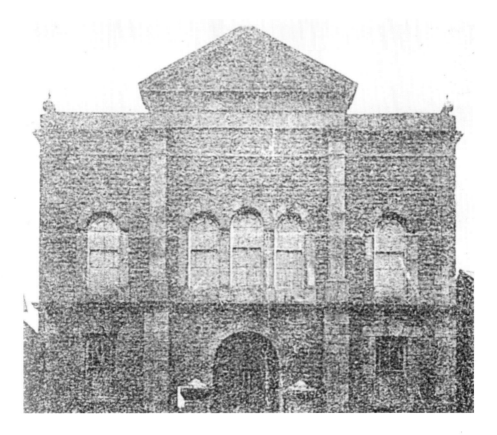

Salem Chapel, 1944

Lt-Col. Montgomery C. Jackson (left) and Officers from the 487 Port Battalion who attended the Reception Concert held at Salem Chapel, Llwynypia, Rhondda, on Monday May 22nd 1944

Troop Concert in Clydach Vale Rhondda Leader June 3rd, 1944
At the music room in the Bush Hotel, Blaenclydach last week a concert was held for Allied forces in the locality. Mr D.J. Evans presided and with Idris Evans at the piano a good evening was assured.

Soloists were Mr. and Mrs. W. Davies, Mr. and Mrs. Will Evans (mechanic), W. Price, David Price, Joe Powell, E.E. Chick, Gwen Gregory, Mrs. Thomas (Bush) and some of the guests.

Addresses of welcome were given by Capt. F.O. Thomas and our local correspondent Mr. D.J. Evans.

With the American troops now settled in throughout the area arrangements had to be made to maintain their general fitness and provide them with the opportunities for physical recreational activities in sports such as baseball. The Minutes of the Rhondda Urban District Council provide evidence of this.

School Management Committee May 17th 1944.

The Director reported that he had been approached by the Officers of the American Troops now stationed in the area regarding the use of the Authority's Mid-Rhondda Athletic Ground for the purpose of physical training and recreation for the troops more particularly those stationed in the Mid-Rhondda Area and also making application for the use of shower baths thereat on the understanding that they would not interfere with the schools now using the field.

The Committee having considered the matter at some length together with the possibility of troops using the King George's Field and the Shower Baths at the Gelligaled Swimming Pool it was Recommended – That the matter be referred to the Members for the Nos. 5, 6 and 7 Wards, the Clerk, the Director and Surveyor to deal with.

CHAPTER 10

The American Army in Penygraig

Penygraig and the immediate surrounding area was home to the 799th Port Company, 517 Port Battalion. The U.S. troops were billeted in homes in most streets in the town.

Provision for feeding the troops were centred on St. Barnabas Church and Llanfair Church. In the halls of both churches cookhouses were established. At St. Barnabas additional structures were built onto the hall to provide toilets and cooking facilities. Every morning soldiers from the surrounding streets would assemble for roll call, then would be fed in the hall itself. Trestle tables and a kettle survive from those days and are still in use.

In Llanfair Church hall a cookhouse was established and two mobile baths were placed in the church grounds for washing facilities.

An armoury was set up in what was relatively recently Colliers shoe shop. Here weapons were stored under armed guard.

Preparations for their arrival had been made early in the year. A report in the Rhondda Leader gives the details.

Rhondda Leader January 29th 1944
Anglo-American Committee. A meeting was convened by Councillor T.H. Thomas at Tabor Vestry, Penygraig, with a view of forming an Anglo-American Forces Reception Committee for Ward 7. There was a representative attendance from Churches, Red Cross, W.V.S., Labour Organisations, Home Guards and Police Force. The Committee officials were elected. Chairman Councillor T.B. Thomas, Secretary, Mr D. Hugh, Indoor Tournaments Committee Mr. W.R. Davies (Chairman) Rev. D. Rees, Rev. R.A. Lewis, Vicar of Williamstown, Messrs. Jack Landeg, A. Rees, T. Shallish, Mrs. H. Dogget, Mrs. Stevens, W.J. Thompson, E.J. Jones and T. Saunders (Secretary).

Outdoors Tournaments – Rev. D. Rees (Chairman), Messrs. W. Springsguth (Secretary), R.G. Henshaw, M. Timmins, T. Shallish, E. Jones, Fred Adams and the Rev. R.A. Lewis.

Ladies Committee – Mrs. E. Jones (Chairman) and Mrs. A. Howells and a group of local ladies.

A reception has been arranged at a local chapel. The Williamstown Gleemen will provide a musical programme and Mr. W.H. Mainwaring M.P. will extend the welcome together with the officials of the Anglo-American Committee.

The American troops did not arrive in the area until early May. Virtually overnight the local scene changed dramatically. The soldiers were quickly and efficiently billeted in local homes and started to get used to the area and mix socially. They were members of the Transportation Corps and jeeps and the big American Army trucks became a common sight in the streets of Penygraig. A tented encampment was set up on the Penygraig Welfare Recreation Ground for training purposes.

After their evening meal in St.Barnabas and Llanfair Church the Americans would gather in crowds in the main street of Penygraig. They always had plenty of company with swarms of children pestering them for gum. The local girls gathered to chat to them. Jill Walters recalls,

"There seemed to be American soldiers everywhere in Penygraig. When we got talking to them we would tease them that many of them had girls names such as Marian, Ira and Gene. They would take it in good part."

The G.I.s mixed socially with their hosts and went down to the local clubs and pubs. They were invited to the Penygraig Conservative and Labour Clubs. The Swan, Butcher's Arms, Turberville and White Rock were popular. Only the last two pubs now remain.

Peggy Gay remembers the two G.I.s who stayed with her family in Mikado Street, Penygraig, had the run of the house. They were very generous and would take all the family to the cinema.

This rosy bonhomie did not exist everywhere. "We'll keep a Welcome in the Hillsides" did not apply at Milbourne Street, Penygraig recalls Professor Eric Talbot. "My father objected to having soldiers compulsorily billeted on him. No way was there going to be wine, women and song as far as he was concerned. Three unfortunate G.I.s were left on his doorstep. He refused to give them a key and insisted they were to be in by 9.30p.m. and definitely no drink. Needless to say I was the only child in the Rhondda who never got any gum or candy. The three camp beds they delivered cluttered up the house for years afterwards."

The Rhondda Leader dated May 27th 1944 gives a picture of the social events taking place.

Rhondda Leader May 27th 1944

A Warm Welcome. Penygraig and district has given Allied troops a warm welcome. Several functions have been arranged locally and there was community singing at Belle Vue Park last Sunday night. An invitation dance was held at Judges Hall, Trealaw on Tuesday night while the Allied troops will give a demonstration of baseball at Mid-Rhondda Grounds on Whit-Monday when the Cossacks pay a visit with their fancy riding in aid of charity.

On the Whit-Monday on a glorious summer's day the famous Russian horsemen thrilled a crowd of over 15,000. The baseball display by teams of American troops took place with loudspeaker commentary by Sgt. Thro.

Local children were interested in watching this new game of baseball. Megan Jones liked to watch the American soldiers playing baseball on Penrhiwfer playing fields.

Another popular pastime among off-duty G.I.s was to wait for the Arsenal train to come into Penygraig station which would be full of female workers to try and arrange dates.

The Arsenal, the Royal Ordnance Factory at Waterton, Bridgend, was one of the largest munition filling factories in Britain. There were 28,000 people working there including several thousand from the Rhondda. Janet Rawlings worked there at that time. She recalls the work was unpleasant and dangerous and accidents were frequent and on some occasions fatal. She herself suffered hand and eye injuries while working on detonators.

Initially there were two shifts, a night shift and a day shift working 8 to 8 alternately. Things improved when a three shift system was introduced.

A day shift for six days, then five afternoon and five night shifts. To catch the morning shift she and hundreds of others had to catch the 5a.m. train from Penygraig to Bridgend. Later a bus service was introduced which made life easier for those living several miles from the station.

Penygraig railway station as it would have looked in 1944. Joan Goddard was the first signalwoman to be appointed in Glamorgan and was in charge of the signalbox shown right. The "March Past" took place on the opposite platform.

THE SIGNAL BOX

For Joan Goddard it was an ordinary night shift as signalwoman at Penygraig railway station.Situated high on the mountainside it had a panoramic view of the valley and the hundreds of houses huddled below. It was 1944 so there were no lights visible from these many homes.The Blackout was strictly enforced.

Among her duties was the control of the coal trains from the collieries at Clydach Vale about three miles up the valley. The first passenger train was the 5a.m. Arsenal train. Hundreds of women from the surrounding areas of Tonypandy, Penygraig, Williamstown and Edmonstown travelled daily to the munition works at the Royal Ordnance Factory in Bridgénd.

Despite being early May the nights were chilly and damp. The stove was unlit and Joan had wrapped a blanket around herself to keep warm. As she waited for the next train she gazed out into the gloom of the night and gradually as the day lightened she could make out the sleeping forms of soldiers lying along the railway embankments. These were the local American troops being toughened up for the events to come.

Suddenly some commands were shouted out and the soldiers moved down on to the railway tracks and eventually formed up into a column on the far end of the opposite platform. To get a better view Joan, still wrapped in her blanket, stood in the open door of the signalbox. The column moved off and came up the platform towards her. To a muffled order their step smartened up and as they drew level to her the commanding officer gave the order "Eyes left". All heads turned smartly and the officers saluted as they marched past. The column of soldiers turned right as they left the station and made their way down into Penygraig.

AN AMERICAN SOLDIER
Remembered by Bryan Williams

In 1944 I was sixteen years of age. We had an American soldier billeted with us in the family home in Vicarage Road, Penygraig. He was Staff Sergeant Vincent Hendrie.

He was tall, clean shaven and well turned out. He slept in our front bedroom and the room had an aroma of aftershave and cigars.

He had a modern personal radio with an extending chrome aerial very much like today's transistors on which he listened to A.F.N., the American Forces Network. I remember he had packs of Chesterfields and Philip Morris cigarettes. He also brought us several cartons of K Rations which contained small tins of bacon and ham, which could be heated, also biscuits, jam, small tins of fruit, chocolate and cigarettes.

He was a very likeable person and got on well with my family and myself. He told us he joined the Army in the winter and sold ice-cream in the summer months. The Americans had an armoury in what was to become in later years Collier's Shoe Shop. I would visit there with Vincent Hendrie. In the armoury the G.I.s on guard would demonstrate their arms drill with the M. 1 Carbine and show me how to bring the rifle to an "On Guard" position from it being slung over their shoulder. I was very impressed.

The G.I.s appeared very young only a little older than myself. Vincent Hendrie appeared to be a father figure to them.

We had a letter from Belgium dated February 25th 1945 in which he said he might get leave and if so would call up to Penygraig to renew contact and pick up his dress uniform and personal effects. Nothing was heard from him again and we feared the worst.

He appeared to be a very caring person and in his letter warned my father to keep me away from firearms remembering my interest in the armoury. His dress uniform hung in the wardrobe for years. I cannot recall what happened to it or his personal possessions.

The troops moved out so quickly that everything was just left. I sometimes wonder what happened to him. I still have his last letter.

(Author's note.
Staff Sergeant Vincent Hendrie survived the war. He was in the Regular Army and was a sergeant in the Infantry for twelve years before joining the 517 Port Battalion. He finished his wartime duty on September 1st 1945 and then re-enlisted in the Army Air Force on the 7th October 1947.)

Somewhere in Belgium
799th Port Co. 517 Port Battalion
A.P.O. 228 U.S. Army
25th February 1945

Dear Jack,

I suppose you wonder sometimes whether I am alive but I can assure you I am very much alive and hope to stay that way. Never one for writing, I hope you do not think my neglect in not writing means that I've forgot about you, as I think quite often of you all and wonder how you're making out with the buzz bombs, evacuees and all.

I suppose Mrs. Williams is kept busy as usual and do hope she is well.
Well Jack it looks like we hoped the finish of things over here a little previously and its not that we're not doing a good job of it, but the Jerries are hanging on tenaciously, but all things must come to an end sometime and I really believe the end is in sight. With his source of supply being cut down each day he'll have to fold up, no matter how.

They have started giving us leave to the U.K. now and I think I have a pretty good chance of getting one the latter part of March or the First of April. I intend to stay in Barry but I shall certainly pay you and your family a visit. I was wondering if Mrs. Williams had held on to my clothes, especially the coat and peaked cap, as they would come in pretty handy while I am there.

Captain Dunbar left the company in September and I understand he is in England now, maybe he has paid a visit to Penygraig by now.

Well Jack, as you well know the censorship prohibits any discussion of my activities over here, so I'll save all that until I see you all. My family is well and my brother has recovered from his illness and graduated from school. He is now doing research work in the Signal Corps Laboratories near our home.

I hope you can find time to answer this short note as I would certainly like to hear how you and yours are. I hope you will forgive me, but I can't remember your young son's name, but anyway my best to him and I hope he is being careful with firearms.

Best regards to the Mrs.
Sincerely Vincent Hendrie

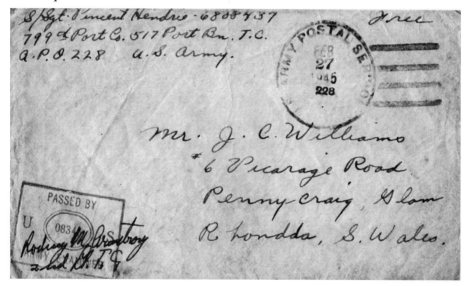

Copy of Envelope sent by Vincent Hendrie

Tec. 4 Chester K. Kastava was a member of the 799ᵗʰ Port Company, 517 Port Battalion. Commanded by Captain Philo V. Dunbar the 3 officers and 232 men were billeted in Penygraig. As part of 5ᵗʰ Engineer Special Brigade they had undergone training at the Amphibious Training School at Mumbles, Swansea. They were to land on Omaha Beach on D-Day June 6ᵗʰ 1944 and suffered many casualties. Tec. Kastava is wearing the shoulder patch of the Army Amphibious Units.

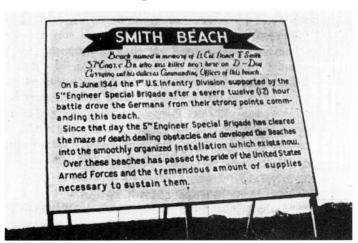

Notice on Smith Beach
The 487 Port Battalion was a unit in this 5th Engineer Special Brigade

The 799th Port Company of the 517 Port Battalion was billeted in Penygraig in May1944. Sgt Albert P. Quarrtararo (on the right) and his two companions were members of this Company. The 799th Company had been based at Hayes Lane Camp since March 1943 discharging cargo at Barry Docks. The photographs illustrate some of their activities.

THE HOME GUARD

On May the 14th 1940 Anthony Eden spoke on the radio. He was in charge of the War Office. "We want large numbers of men between the ages of seventeen and sixty-five." These men would defend Britain. They would be trained to fight. A man could join at the local police station.

Men rushed to stations all over Britain. A quarter of a million men joined on the first day. The Home Guard was formed.

Initially known as the L.D.V. the Local Defence Volunteers the title was soon changed to the Home Guard. In the early days they lacked weapons and uniforms. By 1943 it was an efficient fighting force of nearly two million men.

There were Home Guard Detachments in virtually every town in the Rhondda numbering in total some six hundred men. In the Penygraig-Williamstown area there was even a mounted unit. On their horses they could patrol the mountain tops on the lookout for German paratroopers or baled out enemy airmen.

The photograph shows one of the Home Guard units. It was No 1 Platoon (Penygraig) E Company, 7th Glamorgan Battalion. The Captain (sixth to the right second row) was Emrys Davies, a well known local printer. The man to his left was Lieutenant Trevor Griffiths, the manager of the Penygraig Co-operative clothing department. Other men included in the photograph are, John Davies, Ivor Davies, Cliff Banfield, Enoch Evans, Dennis Banfield, Jack Griffiths, Eddie Pugsley, Danny Jones, George Mumford, Danny Harris, Phillip Thomas, Bill Llewellyn, Bryn Jones, Idris Jones, Dai Taylor, Jack Kington, Will Wellington Dai Phillips, Mike Foley, Evan Ashford, Joe Meadon, Kingsley Davies, Teddy Foley, Evan Jones, William John Jones and Joe(Bach)Lewis.
Some of the Home Guard units took part in exercises with the American forces in the Rhondda. They formed the "enemy" forces to the GIs..

Now at last the plans drawn up to welcome the Americans to Penygraig could be put into action. The 799th Port Company of the 517 Port Battalion were invited to a public reception held at Soar Chapel, Penygraig. A full report of the event was reported in the local press.
Rhondda Leader June 3rd 1944

Allied Forces Welcome

At a function held at Soar Chapel, Penygraig, on Tuesday evening a public reception was given to our Allied Forces. Mr. W.R. Davies presided.

An official welcome was extended by Councillor Evan Oakley, T.B. Thomas, Mrs .E. Jones and the Vicar of Llanfair the Rev. M. Rees. An official response was made by Lt-Colonel Harold E. Bonar, Captain Dunbar and Lt-Chaplain W.W. Anzani.

Entertainment was provided by the Williamstown Gleemen with Miss Mary Carpenter as conductor and organist assisted by Mme. Bessie Jones (soprano) W. Griffiths, Gilfach Goch (baritone) and Mr James Griffiths(tenor).

The evening had been a tremendous success and local organisations looked forward to further events.

This was not to be, the following day the American troops received orders to move out. The historic invasion of France, D-Day was only days away. The 799th Port Company as part of 6th Engineer Special Brigade was to land on Omaha Beach on the 6th June.

Soar Chapel, Penygraig
A welcome reception was held here on May 30th 1944

CHAPTER 11

The American troops in the Upper Rhondda Fawr

The buildup of American troops continued with the arrival of the 185th Port Company of the 487 Port Battalion on May 17th 1944. They travelled by train to Pentre from Newport.

Advance troops had arrived in late April and had been billeted in Maindy Barracks in Pentre the former home of the local Territorial Regiment. Mrs Mary Davies can remember the date of the G.I.s being here more clearly than most. It was a common practice at that time, when the birth of a baby was imminent, for the expectant mother to return to her parents' home. The confinement would then take place in the front room. Being the best room in the house it would be suitable to receive visitors wishing to see the new arrival. On May 11th 1944 her new son arrived. Outside, in the street, American soldiers were sitting on the windowsills and pavement. Every morning they would assemble there ready to form up to be marched down to the feeding centre. A sergeant arrived and with a few orders they got into formation and marched off to breakfast. As she nursed her new born son she said she thought of the mothers of those young soldiers outside and hoped that her new baby would never have to go through times like that.

In Pentre and Treorchy a Police Sergeant Moore saw to the billeting of the troops. He was typical of the local police who knew the area like the back of their hands and saw to the smooth running of the pre-arranged plans. He was one of the joint co-ordinators with Lieut. Colonel John Evans J.P. for the reception committee to welcome U.S. troops.

The soldiers were billeted in homes from Ton Pentre and Y2 Pentre up through Treorchy to Treherbert. Pentre had been selected as the administrative centre for this area. Advance detachments had constructed a Nissen Hut to serve as a cookhouse to the rear of the British Legion in Pentre. The Legion was the feeding centre for the area which included Treorchy. The Pentre Hotel became the local H.Q. and Pay Office. American G.M.C. and Dodge trucks ferried goods and personnel about the area.

The local reception committee was at last able to put its long arranged plans into action and this event was recorded in the local press.

Lt-Col M.C. Jackson (left) and Company Commanders of the 487 Port Battalion. This Battalion of over a thousand men was billeted in the Rhondda Fawr.

Officers of the 186 Port Company billeted in Treherbert with the Battalion Chaplain. Lt Gensch, Lt Amos, Lt Chaplain Whley and Lt Spicuzza

Although the American troops were billeted in private homes, this was for sleeping purposes only. During the day they occupied and trained in tented encampments. This photogrpah shows the 487 Port Battalion camped north of Newport. This camp was later moved and erected in Eileen Place Park, Treherbert.

Rhondda Leader June 3rd 1944
Ton Pentre
A reception concert for Allied troops was held in the Workmans Hall, Ton Pentre on Sunday evening May 28th. The troops turned up in force and thoroughly enjoyed the musical programme provided by the Cory Workmens Prize Band (conducted by Mr. Reg Little) and emminent artistes.

Lieut. Colonel D.G. Richards who took over the duties of M.C. called upon the Band to open the programme with the Allied troops national anthem. Lieut. Colonel Richards then welcomed the Allied troops to the district and Mr. Tom Breacher (Chairman of the Institute) spoke in similar vein.

The audience was called upon to welcome them and the favourite hymn "Cwm Rhondda" was sung with great fervour and the American chorus "John Brown's Body."

Responding to the welcome Lieut. Brown representing Colonel Jackson said he was overjoyed at the warmth of the welcome he had received in the district. He was also speaking for his men when he said they had never received before such a warm and homely welcome. Sgt. Thro representing Captain Boocock said he fully endorsed the remarks of Lieut. Brown and he could assure them they would never forget their enjoyable stay in the Rhondda.

Cory Band
Back row left to right: Dick Jones, Emlyn Bryant, Don Hendy, Stan Williams, Dilwyn
Davies, John Trotman, Gwyn Davies, Stan Brown, Jim Edwards.
Middle row: Gwyn Davies, George Roderick, Charles Smith, Tommy Roberts, Steve Trotman,
William Lane, Arthur Bryant, Ossie John, Dick Davies.
Front row: Idwal Jenkins, Tom Trotman, Bill Davies, Reg Little, Jack Coombes, Eddie Moore,
Caradoc Davies.

This letter was written by Pfc Arthur Bonner, 185 Port Company, 487 Port Battalion, to his mother in New Jersey, U.S.A..He describes his impression of life in the Rhondda.

41 Troedyrhiw Terrace,
Treorchy, Glam.
March 13ᵗʰ 1945
Dearest Mom,

I'm sure this letter will surprise you. As you know by now I am really getting a real rest here. Ill be leaving here tomorrow morning at 6:00 A.M. It is just too bad that the furlough didn't last a bit longer but I guess I should be thankful for this.
I didn't expect to be so lucky. They had a drawing for three of us. And I guess God was with me. I hope the next furlough I get will be to the U.S.A.

These people were very kind, after all their food is very scarce. Their house is small but still they enjoy life. They are not like the ordinary type of English people. You remember I always disliked the English. The distinction is they are Welsh. People here are all coalminers or factory workers. They were the hardest hit in the early 30's. There is not much entertainment here just a few movies and churches, stores and each bar is called a Pub. That means a place where people gather to drink a few pints of beer and talk. The very well known one here is, "The Red Cow". There you will find some very fine talent for singing.

The mountains here are high and barren. There is not much of anything here compared to home. The thing that makes most of us come back though is that people were so kind and willing. They gave us the key and let us do as they would have their own sons do. Most of all the fellows in the Company have said this was the best place they ever had except for home.

There are five living here in a house that takes up less space than our two front rooms and a pantry. There is Mr. and Mrs. Exell, Gordon is only 18 and is a very fine fellow. He wants to be a flier: women and other things don't enter his mind. He might have to go to the Army, I'm not sure, he has a slight physical disability. Martha is a very fine young girl of 21. She likes children very much and knows how to take care of a house. The lucky man to have her is in the Tank Corps but he has a physical disability so he can't go overseas. They will be married on May the 7th, so please drop a card.

Then there is Mavis, 11, she is quiet and going to school, a very nice child. The cat called "Ginger" is extremely intelligent. The house is heated by a fireplace and that is the kitchen stove. Yes these people live crowded but still very clean.

To give you an idea what they are going through, they get 18 clothing stamps per person. Now all clothing, rugs, towels, curtains and such must be bought out of that. It takes 16 stamps for a pair of shoes, so that's one pair a year, two for a towel, 1/4 of one for a handkerchief. However they get enough food, it is very scarce but not too bad. There is a pretty bad black market. They get 600 pounds of coal a month.

Well must close now, so Mrs. Exell will send you some pictures. I hope you get them alright.

May God Bless You

Lots of Love and Kisses

Arthur

The Pentre Inn 1944
The 487 Port Battalion was billeted in the Rhondda Fawr in an area extending from Tonypandy north to Treherbert. The Commanding Officer Lt. Col. Montgomery C. Jackson had his Headquarters and Battalion Pay Office in the Pentre Inn. This hotel and the Griffen Hotel were billets for officers from the Battalion.

The Red Cow, Treorchy 1944
"There is not much entertainment here just a few movies and small churches and stores and each bar is called a Pub. That means a place where people gather together to drink a few pints of Beer and talk. A very well known one here is the "Red Cow" where you find some very fine talent for singing."
(An extract taken from a letter written home from a G.I. Arthur Bonner to his folks in New Jersey, U.S.A.)

G.I.s were supplied with a pup tent which provided a basic shelter when they were out in the field. Janet Rawlings can remember one Company camped on Dinas Isaf farm, Trebanog in appalling weather. Days of continuous rain had turned the campsite into a mudbath. The "Pup" tents all leaked terribly. (Pfc. Benjamin Gurdison 186 Port Company)

Stuart Street, Treorchy May 1944, viewed from an American Army truck belonging to the 487 Port Battalion.

Vincent Gasperini Karl Gaber Ben Fialkowski Jose Sanchez
186 Port Company 487 Port Battalion U.S. Army
This group of American servicemen billeted in Treherbert was typical of the majority of the 3,000
G.I.s in the Rhondda area in 1944. They were mainly in their late teens or early twenties. They
were given a great welcome and enjoyed the social life on offer.

Rhondda Leader Report Saturday May 27th *1944*
Band Sunday-Cwmparc Church Parade

   A heartfelt appeal to all peoples of the Christian faith to realise the value of prayer was made by Captain Edward L. Reiff (Chaplain to the U.S. Forces in this country) when he addressed a congregation that taxed the seating capacity of Bethal (E.B.) Chapel last Sunday afternoon.

   It was Band Sunday and a parade composed of B Company Home Guards, A.R.P. Wardens, St. John ambulance nurses, cadets and men with Major D.J. Davies as marshall attended. They were headed by the Parc and Dare Workmens Band (bandmaster Hayden Bebb) and the Junior Band (bandmaster Matt Evans). Prior to the service the procession paraded to the top of the district to stirring marches played by both bands. In the chapel they were welcomed on behalf of the pastor, deacons and congregation by Mr. J. O'Brian, Mr. J.H. Lewis presided at the organ and Mr. James Jones acted as precentor.

   Captain Rieff based his address on a verse from the Second Book of Chronicles – "If my people who are called in my name shall humble themselves and seek my face and turn from their wicked ways then I will hear from heaven, forgive their sin and will heal their land."

In Treorchy the Americans enjoyed the same welcome as elsewhere in the Rhondda.

Angela Sidoli remembers them well. For many years her father kept a cafe in High Street, Treorchy. A considerable number of the G.I.s were of Italian descent and made a beeline to the many Italian cafes in the Rhondda.

In addition there were many of Polish descent and on Sunday mornings there were the regular church parades of American soldiers to the Catholic churches in the Valleys.

It was at Sunday Mass at the Immaculate Conception Roman Catholic Church in Treorchy that her family met the soldiers. After Church these G.I.s a mixture of Poles and Italians would come back to her home and crowd into the kitchen at the rear of the shop.

When they discovered the ice-cream making machinery they became very enthusiastic about the possibility of putting it to use. With the wartime shortages all ice-cream making had ceased. The Americans said they could get hold of all the ingredients. Angela recalls "My father said it was against the law to produce ice-cream and he was afraid to get into trouble with the authorities."

Sgt. Moore was consulted and after he had made some discreet enquiries ice-cream production was commenced. Sgt. Moore was well known and a good friend to the local American servicemen. He had organised their billeting and was joint co-ordinator with Lt. Col. John Evans J.P. on the area Reception Committee.

The ice-cream produced was supplied to the American troops billeted in Pentre Barracks and to the feeding station at Pentre Legion. Her father was amazed at the amount and variety of the ingredients. Canned fruit which had long disappeared from local shops was to be had in abundance, sugar and milk was plentiful. There was always some surplus ice-cream and a large tub of it would be carried out into the street by the G.I.s and shared out to eager local children.

She recalls the name of only one of the G.I.s, a Sgt. Pat Clancy from New York, the Polish names were too difficult to pronounce.

On Tuesdays and Saturdays the Americans went dancing to the Boys Club in Treorchy.

Treherbert played its part in this American story. Situated at the head of the Rhondda Fawr and backed by the rugged Rhigos Mountain it presented a scenic environment for the Company of American troops billeted in the long terraced streets.

Once news of the impending arrival was given, the local people took action. A report in the local press illustrates the spirit of the times.

Rhondda Leader Report January 29ᵗʰ 1944

Good progress is being made by the committee set up by the Free Church Council to make the necessary arrangements for the welcoming of the American troops expected in the locality shortly. This was the first committee set up in the valley and has been fortunate in obtaining the use of the rooms of the old Dandy Club, Bute Square, through the kindness of the local Home Guard and the owners Mr. and Mrs. Cule.

Several sub-committees have been set up for the entertainment of the troops. It is hoped that when the men arrive a public meeting will be held to give them a welcome and to this all residents will be heartily invited.

The ladies are responsible for the canteen and will be glad of further assistance. Mrs. Phelps, St. Albans Road is the convener of the committee. Mr. Levi Poole has been placed in charge of the library and Mr. T. Emmanuel appointed to assist him.

The officers of the committee are the Rev. R.T .Davies B.A. (Chairman), Mr. J.L. Haddock (Treasurer) and Mr. J.R. Edwards (General Secretary).

The sub-committee set up has been very busy indeed in colouring the walls, cleaning the rooms generally and getting the rooms into decent order for the visitors. Members of the Cymric Club have loaned the committee several articles of furniture. It is very gratifying to note that the churches are taking such a live interest in the matter and are contributing to the expense. The committee would be glad to receive copies of periodicals when the men arrive. Table tennis balls would also be welcome.

Prior to the arrival of the main body of troops advance parties of American servicemen had constructed a Nissen Hut in Taff Street on land adjoining the Cymric Club or Band Room as it was sometimes known. This was fitted out with stoves and trestle tables and was to be used as a cookhouse and feeding station. The local H.Q. was to be the Cymric Club.

On May 15ᵗʰ 1944 the 186 Port Company of the 487 Port Battalion arrived in Treherbert. They had been conveyed there in American G.M.C. trucks from their former base in Newport, Gwent.

In charge of the Company was Captain Clifford J. Anderson and three officers 1ˢᵗ Lt Frank E. Amis, 1ˢᵗ Lt. Robert H. Gensch and 2ⁿᵈ Lt. Frank A. Spicuzza. They were in charge of 238 Enlisted Men.

Treherbert took on the air of a garrison town. The Bwlch and Rhigos Mountains were used for training purposes not only by troops of the 487 Port Battalion but also those of the Second Infantry Division from their encampment down in the Craig-Y-Llyn basin. There was the constant traffic of military vehicles, trucks, jeeps, weapons carriers and Dodge ambulances.

Columns of troops laden with their weapons and gear marched through the town and then toiled up the steep mountain roads. There were many tented camps set up, the main encampment was in Eileen Place Park. In the evening uniformed off-duty soldiers were much in evidence.

A permanent tented camp was set up in the basin of Craig-Y-Llyn. This well known glaciated feature contained a lake and is backed by precipitous cliffs and in 1944 was not forested. This was a training camp for the American infantry. The whole area was an exclusion zone with road blocks manned by armed guards. There were reports of troops scaling the high cliffs and talk of American Rangers, the equivalent of British commandos, training in the area.

It was a time of strict security and rumours abounded and some still linger on today. With the passage of time and the rules of wartime secrecy some events will remain shrouded in mystery. At one period buses taking munitions workers to the explosives factory at Hirwaun from the Rhondda travelled with curtained windows.

Firing ranges were set up on the mountain and these were like magnets to some children who collected empty ammunition cartridge cases. Despite guards being posted children got access to these dangerous areas. In the Rhondda and on the Treforest ranges children were killed and injured. Children were warned in schools, there were special talks, posters displayed, and in the cinema short government films with frightening scenes shown. All warned children and adults to leave any metal objects found on the ground well alone.

Almost home... Weary Troops of the 487 Port Battalion wind their way down the sheeptracks to the valley below and home to their billets. They were at the end of a 25 mile route march.

*American troops of the 487 Port Battalion stand silhoueted
against the mist filled Rhondda Valley.*

Pvt. Arthur Bonner of the 185 Port Company was staying with Gordon
Exell's parents in Treorchy

He recalls that Pvt.Bonner returned home in the late afternoon so
exhausted by the 25 mile hike that he was hardly able to stand. Retiring
to his bed he slept through the next day, which was a Sunday, getting up
on the Monday morning. His parents were worried by him sleeping so
long.

*"Our time there (in the Rhondda) was spent marching up and down the
mountains during the day." Pfc Benjamin Gurdison, 186 Port Company.*

When the American troops were training on the Rhondda mountains a welcome sight was the arrival of the mobile field kitchen.

Roy Jones from Treherbert remembers such an event.

"I was up on the Rhigos Mountain with my friends watching the American soldiers training They were resting by the roadside when a mobile kitchen arrived towed by a big truck. The soldiers formed a queue and received their food doled out into sectioned metal trays. When the sat down on the grass verges their food had all run together, their custard ran into their gravy. It didn't seem to bother them and they ate it all the same."

U.S Army Mobile Field Kitchen

On the social scene the troops mixed well with the local population. Particularly popular were the dances held at the Lido, a dancehall belonging to the Tynewydd Labour Club. Here dancers were entertained by the Evie Davies Dance Band.

The Evie Davies Quintet at the Tynewydd Labour club in 1944. The band members Tommy French, Bob Green (drums), Dai Squires (piano) Randall Covey (violin) and Evie Davies (sax). Others pictured include Walter Locket, Gwynfor Evans, Alwyn Evans, John Morgan, Eileen Locket, Dilys Evans, Jean Morgan and Bob Morgan. The Lido dancehall attached to the club was popular with the local GIs and in addition every Wednesday a convoy of trucks brought solders from the U.S. Secondary Infantry Division to the dance. They were based in a tented training camp in the basin of the Llyn Fawr.

Before joining the Army, Ernie Fair at the age of seventeen was a drummer in this band. He recalls the band tried to keep up-to-date and played items by Glen Miller and Tommy Dorsey as well as the traditional tangos and foxtrots. In the intervals the music of Glen Miller was played on records.

Every Wednesday night troops from the infantry camp up in the Craig-y-Llyn would arrive by truck to increase the American presence. Jitterbugging was the new dance craze and the G.I.s attempted to show how it was done.

A formal welcome planned as far back as January 1944 was at last carried out.

Rhondda Leader Report June 3rd 1944

Treherbert. A reception meeting for Allied troops was held at Bethany E.B. Church on Sunday evening May 28th. Community singing was indulged in and the Blaencwm Choral Society (conducted by Mr. J. Hayden Davies) contributed items. Solos were rendered by Miss Iris Anfield and Mr. D. Davies and a recitation by Mr. R. Prysor Williams. Mr. J. Bennet proved an efficient accompanist. The Rev. R.T.S. Davies presided.

Mrs Iris Evans who as the 20 year old Iris Anfield sang at the concert remembers there was a wonderful atmosphere and the Chapel was packed to the doors. John Hayden Davies was a marvellous conductor and the Blaencwm Choir provided a first class performance. The American contingent was overwhelmed by the welcome.

Miss Anfield sang in many concerts at this time entertaining wounded American and British servicemen at Whitchurch and Rhydlafar Hospitals.

A reception meeting for the American troops in Treherbert was held at Bethany E.B Church on Sunday evening May 28th 1944.

MEMORIES FROM 1944

"*They had camped with small pup tents on Dinas Isaf Farm. It was very wet and cold and the site was very muddy. They stood in groups outside the Black Diamond in Edmondstown soaking wet and looking miserable. We invited them back to our homes to cheer them up.*" Muriel Thomas

"*Two American soldiers were billeted with my parents in Eirw Road, Porth. An American padre would visit my home to enquire about their behaviour. We had no complaints about them, quite the reverse, they were pleasant, well mannered and generous.*" Megan Webb

"*I was on leave from the Royal Artillery and hearing that the Americans had set up a range on the Nant above Cwmparc I went up there. The area was under armed guard. I got talking to one of the G.I.s on guard and seeing that I was in the Army he escorted me up to the range to see what was going on. They were firing Bangalore torpedoes and mortars. They were Rangers, a combat unit and a tough looking lot.*" Chris Phillips

"*Every Wednesday evening the American troops camped by the Llyn would come down to the dance in the Lido in Treherbert. They would arrive in a convoy of American trucks.*

I was asked to dance by one G.I. and he tried to jitterbug to a Gypsy Tango. When they put on Glen Miller records during the interval the Yanks showed how it should be done. Jiving was a craze and very popular with the girls." Christine Fair

"*My mother was cleaning the upstairs windows of our home in Primrose Street, Tonypandy. With the old sash windows you sat on the sill to clean the top section. Gilbert White who was billeted with us was marching down the street with a column of soldiers, when he saw my mother clinging on to the window. He shouted up "Watch you don't fall Mrs. Jones" and all the rest of the soldiers sang in a chorus the same warning over and over again like a song. My mother went as red as a beetroot.*" Dorothy Jones

"*Bill Rombercich was billeted with us in Thomas Street. He was a cook in the American Army and worked in the cookhouse built next to Zion Chapel near Pandy Square. He always brought meat and other food home for us so we did very well. He was much older than the others in his Company. He said as he was leaving for France that his son was arriving in Britain with an Infantry Division. He sent my daughter his photograph from France.*" Violet Thomas

"A G.I. was dating a girl living in Grawen Street, Porth and every evening he would turn up in a jeep. Two friends and myself were given gum and candy to guard it. On one occasion he gave us a ride up to Garth Park in the jeep which was a great thrill.

One evening we turned up as usual but he and the jeep did not. We learned that the Americans had left the area and would not be coming back. We were very disappointed at this news." Terry Blinkhorn

The G.I.s were very popular with the Rhondda children who soon learnt the expression "Got any Gum, Chum". They were a source of great interest not only for the chewing gum and chocolate they so liberally provided but also for the novelty of talking to men from America the country they saw so often in the local cinemas. The soldiers dressed in their battle gear and carrying weapons and riding about in their jeeps and huge lorries presented an exciting scene, "Just like the Pictures". When the troops marched up the mountain they invariably had a posse of children in tow.

The bulk of the soldiers were in their late teens or early twenties, were generally full of fun, and got on well with the youngsters.

In a letter home Pvt. Arthur Bonner 185th Port Company writes on May 20th 1944. "As you know the children go crazy over Gum and we of course are very generous."

The photograph featured above shows a crowd of children in Taff Street, Treherbert, posing for an American photographer. The photographer 1st Sgt. Wilbert J. Schuman captured for posterity this wartime scene of local children with American troops in the background.
The Band Hut and Nissen Hut in Taff Street served the 186 Port Company as the local H.Q. and feeding station.

Lt. Frank A Spicuzza

With the entry of America into the war there was a great expansion of the Officer Corps. Men were appointed as officers in this "citizen army" on ability not on social background as was the case in the British Army. Lt. Frank A Spicuzza was typical of this new breed of officer. The son of Sicilian immigrants and one of thirteen children he managed despite the hardships of the Depression to graduate as a schoolteacher.

He was an officer in the 186 Port Company of the 487 Port Battalion and was billeted in Treherbert. He was awarded the Bronze Star for the part he played in the Omaha landing.

A government poster campaign urged people to Dig for Victory. Lawns and flowerbeds all over Britain were dug up and transformed into vegetable plots and people began eating produce from their own backyards and allotments.

Suitable sites for cultivation were limited in the Rhondda Valleys because of the steep mountainside. However the efforts of the people of Treherbert so impressed the Americans billeted here that a photographic record was made. This photograph was taken and bore the caption; Victory Gardens, Treherbert, Wales.

Victory Gardens, Treherbert

*Captain Anderson and men from the 186 Port Company billeted in Treherbert
do their bit to help the Welsh food production effort.*

Rhondda Leader Report June 3rd 1944

"People like you are the salt of the earth and are doing a fine job of work for the war effort". This is what Captain Anderson told the street collectors at a meeting held at the British Legion Club on Wednesday 31st May.

Mr. Gorwel Owen, the club Chairman welcomed the street collectors and thanked them for the excellent work which had been put in during the week of the campaign. They were pleased to have among them their allied friends Captain

Anderson and Sgt. Warshansky and he was also glad to seen Inspector Charles Evans present. The secretary Mr. R.W. Greene gave a report on the results achieved. An enjoyable programme arranged by Miss Violet Gibson included community singing conducted by Councillor Ivor I Jones. Solo items were contributed by Sgt. Warshansky, Mrs. K lewis-Lloyd and Mrs. Crad Davies.

The Chairman thanked the British Legion for granting the use of their rooms for the meeting in connection with the campaign in the district.

Little did the local people at this meeting or their American guests suspect that within hours of this event the American troops would be gone from the area and travelling to their embarkation ports for the invasion beaches of Normandy.

Captain Clifford J. Anderson
Captain Anderson was from Montana. He was the Company Commander
of the 186 Port Company, 487 port Battalion billeted in Treherbert.

THE CLOSEST THING TO HOME

Treherbert remembered by Pfc. Benjamin Gurdison, 186 Port Company, 487 Port Battalion, U.S. Army.

Treherbert, Rhondda, South Wales, was an extremely quiet town before our arrival there. This a very small town in the uppermost confines of the Rhondda Valley, which is in the heart of the coal mining section of Wales. It is a beautiful little town set between two huge rows of mountains.

The people there had been waiting on us for nearly three weeks as we were to be spread out all over the town, usually two men to a home. Our hearts really warmed to these people after the welcome we received. They were only too pleased to help us in any manner. Even the small children tried to help us with our luggage as we moved from the trucks to our new home.

Most of the men were considered part of the family by the people where they stayed. Hardly a night would pass without having a chat over a cup of tea, before retiring.

Our time was spent marching up and down the mountains during the day and in the evenings we were invited to parties, dances and we hardly had any time to ourselves. It was strange the way the men grumbled when we hiked up the hills in formation, during the day, but in the evening half of these same men could be seen walking up the same pathway, with their girlfriends.

We were in Treherbert for only 17 days when we were ordered to a staging area for the Invasion.

By far, the leaving of Treherbert hurt us the most. The people were lined on the streets in the morning we left, some even tearful. Truthfully we were as unhappy as they were, as this had been the closest thing to home that we had seen in the Army.

CHAPTER 12

The Americans: The Social Round

The arrival of the American soldiers in the Rhondda as in other parts of Britain formed a great attraction for the female population particularly for teenagers.

This was recognised in official circles with some concern and was summed up in a Home Office Report in 1945.

"The girls brought up on the cinema who copied the dress, hair styles and manners of Hollywood stars, the sudden influx of Americans speaking like the films, who actually lived in the magic country and who had plenty of money at once went to the girls' heads. The American attitude to women, their proneness to spoil a girl, to build up, exaggerate, talk big and act with generosity and flamboyance helped to make the most attractive boyfriends."

The arrival of the Americans caused a great deal of interest on the local scene. It coincided with the excitement of new dances such as jitterbugging or jiving and the arrival of the big band sound. This new music was played constantly on the wireless. The music associated with Artie Shaw, Tommy Dorsey and above all Glen Miller playing romantic "smooth music". For many the memories of the G.I.s is recalled by the music of Glen Miller's signature tune Moonlight Seranade.

In the Rhondda dancehalls local bands copied these popular tunes and in the intervals phonograph records were played featuring the famous bands. Dances were held which featured American Army dance bands. In the Salute the Soldier Week, April 22nd to the 29th a U.S. Army band played in the Judges Hall, Trealaw and in Polikoff's canteen, Treorchy. In the Municiple Town Hall in Pontypridd well known American and British big bands played to packed houses.

Dancing was very popular with all ages. It offered an escape from the wartime austerity and anxieties and it was fun and cheap. Almost every town in the Rhondda had a dancehall, sometimes two or more.

Tonypandy was served by two main dancehalls. There was the Judges Hall in Trealaw and the Library in Llwynypia and other minor halls.

There was dancing every night apart from Sunday. The halls were alcohol free, well managed by responsible people and the towns were well policed.

Youngsters went dancing from the age of fourteen and it was an ideal place for them to enjoy themselves and mix socially. The popularity of the dance halls increased with the arrival of hundreds of young American soldiers and the girls flocked to a dancehall if the GI's were present. The enlisted men were generally in the 18 to 20 age group with some as young as 17. The novelty factor of meeting these young men from the United States was immense, their accents, their smart uniforms and coming from places they had seen in the cinema made them something special. Many went out with them and took them home to meet Mam.

	Trevor Nicholls		Des Wheel		Vocalist Unknown		
Tommy	Ivor	?	Elwyn		Morris	Bryn	Tommy
Lloyd	Owen		Lloyd		Williams	Lloyd	Lewis

The MIlton Mace Band

Chris Wilkins Evan Jnes   Milton Mace   Bill James

Tommy French Tich Hines Tommy Lewis Ianto ? Evan Jones Eddie Dowton Tom Morse

The American Government's generosity and interest in their soldiers welfare contrasted starkly with the British Government's attitude. President Roosevelt had declared "Nothing but the best for our Boys" and this was reflected in the equipment, clothes, pay and provisions for their well being.

It was a criticism that the American troops were overpaid in comparison with their British counterparts. The truth was that the British soldier was grossly underpaid.

The discrepancy in pay was real enough. In June 1943 a private in the British Army was paid 14 shillings a week whereas a private in, the U.S. Army received £3.8s.9d, nearly five times as much.

With almost all food found and a subsidised P.X.(Post Exchange-a kind of government shop stocking an abundance of imported U.S. goods) the G.I. had a considerable disposable income.

Comparing the American P.X. with the British N.A.F.F.I cigarettes were one tenth of the price, superior in quality and virtually unlimited in supply.

The American troops billeted in valley homes saw at first hand the severity of British rationing and would arrive home with cans of peaches, packets of sugar, tins of luncheon meat and corn beef.

In the days when smoking was very fashionable and universally enjoyed the G.I.s hosts enjoyed themselves with the abundance of cigarettes and cigars brought back in the evening.

Gordon Exell of Clarke Street, Treorchy, recalls the two young men staying with his family. Pfc. Arthur Bonner and Sgt. Luckic were both quiet in nature who liked nothing better than sitting by the fireside and talking. Their billet was a home from home. They returned this hospitality with tinned foodstuffs and cigarettes which his father being a heavy smoker particularly valued

The Army authorities noted the British soldiers' resentment at the GIs ability to outspend them and their inferiority complex was increased by the contrast in dress. The British soldier wore an all purpose battledress made of thick coarse wool. This could be worn all day for general military duties and for social activities. The GI had three outfits: fatigues, a jacket and trousers of R.B.T. cotton for rough work, a field service dress of combat clothing and a service jacket and trousers with shirt and tie. The latter was of superior quality and was an enormous social asset for the G.I. in Britain making them look like an officer to the British eye.

To finish of the comparison in dress was the type of footwear worn. The G.I. for social occasions wore rubber soled shoes with leather uppers whereas the Tommies had to wear hob-nailed boots, hardly fashionable for the dance-floor

When the GIs went out on dates they often carried with them cigarettes, sweets and the most valued of all nylons. Amongst the girls these nylons were greatly treasured. Because of the shortage of silk, stockings had disappeared although among working class girls their possession was rare because of their expense. Many girls painted their legs with pancake makeup or even gravy browning using eyebrow pencil to draw in a seam. The gift of nylons made from artificial silk and the wearing of them caused a few raised eyebrows.

A Ferndale lady remembers rushing into her home excitedly clutching a pair of nylons. She had been walked home from a dance in the Rink by a GI who had given them as a gift. She was dismayed to be told off by her father for accepting them and a furious row developed. Her mother's approach was different, "I'll have these," she said, snatching the prize.

Most of the romances were of a transient nature although a number of Rhondda girls married Americans and joined the 70,000 G.I. Brides who settled down to a new life in America.

Great administrative obstacles were placed in the way of potential brides and permission was required from the Commanding Officer of the various military units for a marriage to take place

The marriage and engagement columns of the Rhondda Leader frequently carried announcements similar to the following:

Rhondda Leader - Marriages
Helton-Smith. On April 15th 1945 the marriage took place of Monroe Helton (Sgt. U.S. Army) Kentucky U.S.A. to Mattie, daughter of Mr. and Mrs. Thomas Smith, 17 Jestyn Street, Mount Pleasant, Porth.

Otis-Lloyd. At St. Mary Magdalene R.C. Church on Saturday April 5th 1945 by special licence of Sgt. Eugene (Gene) J. Otis U.S. Army, eldest son of Mr. and Mrs. J. Otis, Forest City, Iowa to Ruth daughter of Mr. and Mrs. Rees Lloyd, 1 William Street, Ynyshir Goul-Phelps.

On Friday 29th April 1945 at Carmel English Congregational Church, Trebanog.

Pte. Robert L .Goul, U.S. Army only son of Mr. and Mrs. C.W. Goul, Ohio, U.S.A. was married to Miss Margaret Phelps, 106 Edmundstown Road, Penygraig. The Rev. Wyn Parry officiated and Mr. Samuel Griffiths presided at the organ.

Engagement.
Saturday June 24th.1944

Hartman-Prosser. Elmore O. Hartman only son of Mr. and Mrs Hartman, Virginia, to Barbara, younger daughter of Mr. and Mrs. W.M. Rosser, Trehafod.

A GI Wedding in Tonypandy... Rhondda Leader Report February 2nd 1945
At St. Raphaels, Tonypandy on January 23rd the marriage took place of S/Sgt Ted. H. Rozniak, U.S. Army, only son of Mr. and Mrs. Michael Rozniak, Buffalo, New York City to L.A.W.C. Margaret Eluned Jones, only child of Mrs. S. Jones and the late Mr. D.C. Brychan Jones (rating officer, R.U.D.C.) Haulfryn, 33 Gilfach Road, Tonypandy. Prior to her enlistment the bride was a member of the clerical staff of Rediffusion Ltd at Tonypandy.

Several members of the bridegroom's unit attended and served in the following order:Best Man, Sgt. Foster Vaughan, Groomsmen, Sgt. Leo McCarthy and Cpl. Edward Vasick, Ushers, Cpl. Orville Arthur, Pts. Edward Powlice and James Crittender.

After the ceremony a reception was held at the house of the bride and about 50 guests assembled. The newly married couple spent their honeymoon in Porthcawl before returning to their respective units.

A WEDDING IN THE SNOW
Remembered by Bryan Morse.

There had been a heavy fall of snow and myself and other children were using our wooden sledges on the steep Gilfach Road hill. There was of course no street lighting and no light from the houses because of the Blackout. Moonlight provided us with a Christmas card scene.

Unknown to us a wedding party was going on in full swing in one of the houses. We were surprised to suddenly have the company of American soldiers from the party. In exchange for sweets and cakes they borrowed our sledges. No doubt somewhat merry from the festivities they hurtled down the long steep hill at breakneck speed with cigars clenched firmly in their mouths. After much shouting, laughing and falling about they struggled back up the hill through the deep snow only to repeat the procedure over and over again. What with the snow, the friendly Americans, the sweets and the cakes, it was an evening we children thoroughly enjoyed.

Photograph taken outside St. Rapaels Church, Tonypandy at the wedding of S/Sgt. Ted. H. Rozniak and Margaret Eluned Jones. The little girl presenting the lucky horseshoe was Gillian Williams.

RHONDDA GIRL BECOMES G.I. BRIDE

This photograph shows Glenys and Chuck Tounzen on their wedding day in Modesta, California in 1947. Glenys met her future husband Chuck when she and a friend visited a fair in Pontypridd in 1944.

Glenys who worked in the canteen of Wattstown Colliery after leaving school said, "Chuck was in the U.S. Army based in Pontypridd and I guess we fell in love there among the dodgems and the carousel."

Glenys lived in Ynys Street in Ynyshir. Chuck went back to his home in Modesta, California in 1945 when the war ended, but the romance blossomed as the couple regularly wrote letters to each other.

In 1947 Glenys decided to leave her home in Ynys Street and join Chuck in the States.

She said, " Mam was not pleased and would not give her permission to get wed but I was determined to go."

She and her husband have regularly visited her sister Joyce Morgan at the family home in Ynys Street. Glenys said, "I have been back home for a holiday during 38 of the 52 years I have lived in California. The Rhondda is my home and I love coming back to see family and friends."

Chuck Tounzen was a member of an anti-air craft battalion which was billeted in various halls in the Pontypridd area in March 1944. They picked up their guns, trucks and other equipment in Pontypridd and from there went to Barmouth, North Wales for test firing and extra training.

They then moved to Manchester to wait for D-Day. Prior to D-Day the battalion moved to Nettlebed in Oxfordshire to waterproof equipment. They departed England from Weymouth July 7th 1944 for Utah Beach in France and were incorporated into the United States Third Army under General Patton.

THE FLOOD

The arrival of the American soldiers into Hopkinsto caused a great deal of interest not least among the young ladies of the village remembers Marion Lewis.

When they passed us in their trucks and jeeps they would whistle and call out. During the day they were away from the area but they returned in the evening to their billets around the village, most were staying in the local church halls.

We were pleased to learn that a dance was going to be held in a local church hall as a welcoming gesture to the Americans. In the war years new clothes were difficult to obtain and we had to save up our clothing coupons and what was available was not very fashionable. It was a matter of make do and mend. Fashion stockings were unavailable and some of the girls used leg make-up or even gravy browning to give the appearance of stockings. I had managed to obtain a pair of green suede shoes. I was very proud of these and I was going to wear them to the dance.

The night of the long awaited dance arrived. The weather had been absolutely awful with several days of heavy rain. Along the mountain- sides the streams had become raging torrents. The night of the dance was no exception, still it poured down. But, with the prospect of a great night ahead my friends and I set out eagerly for the dance, rain or no rain.

The downpour deterred no-one. The church hall was full of young people out to enjoy themselves.

The band had braved the weather and the hall had been transformed with flags and bunting. All was set for a great evening.

The American lads arrived as a group and soon we were all engaged in excited talk with the new arrivals.

When the dance began we took the Americans on to the dance floor. They did not know the various tangos and waltzes and great fun was had trying to teach them. Later on in the evening they were going to teach us how to jitterbug when we had some Glen Miller records, which were all the rage.

All this jollity came to an abrupt end when, with a loud bang, the hall door burst open and a flood of brown muddy water surged into the hall to a depth of two or three feet completely swamping the dance floor. There was a great deal of shouting and not a little panic as dancers slipped and splashed about. There was a general rush for the door and as our new found American friends tried to carry us out through this flood they lost their footing and fell into this filthy brown water. In a matter of minutes everybody was out of the hall, everyone safe but very wet.

The cause of the flood had been the collapse of a culvert to the rear of the church hall and flood water had been diverted into the hall. Soon the flood subsided but the hall was covered with a thick carpet of slime. Among all that debris and probably washed away were my prized green suede shoes.

We all stood outside the hall, soaking wet, dirty and feeling pretty miserable. It was still pouring with rain and with the absence of street lights in the pitch dark. With the aid of the Americans we had befriended, my friends and I made our way back to my family home. When my father opened the door what a sight we presented! Once inside the house my mother sprung into action. Towels and hot water were quickly provided and my girlfriends and I quickly changed into a variety of outfits. The American soldiers were soaked and absolutely filthy. On my mother's orders they removed their outer garments which my mother cleaned as best she could and put them on the range to dry. They donned trousers and other garments belonging to my father, causing much laughter. What a sight they looked.

One of the soldiers seeing how distressed I had been over the loss of my precious shoes had set off back to the church hall and with the aid of his small torch and after much wallowing about in the mud and debris had retrieved my green suede shoes. When he returned and the door was opened he stood in the rain holding the shoes triumphantly, like a true hero.

We all had supper and drank gallons of tea. We talked and laughed for hours reliving the night's events. The Americans told us about their homes so far away in America

The minor disaster of the dance had turned into an unforgetable evening. The friendship and a few parties continued during their brief stay. Then they were gone as if in an instant and we never discovered what happened to them.

The soldiers attending the dance were members of the 509th Parachute Infantry Regiment attached to the 26th Infantry Division billeted in Hopkinstown at that time. It was they who cleaned out the culvert and the hall the following day.

CHAPTER 13

The 94ᵗʰ Medical battalion in Pontypridd

The American presence in the Rhondda was interconnected with Pontypridd. Based at Pontypridd was an U.S. Army Medical Battalion, its official designation was the 94ᵗʰ Air and Rail Evacuation Holding Unit. Officers and enlisted men were billeted in private homes.

An advance party had arrived early in May 1944 and had been working with the Glamorgan Constabulary. Plans had been worked out where the troops were to be billeted. Provisions were made to use two buildings. One was the British Legion and the other a local church. They were to be used as feeding stations and indoor meeting areas.

The main body of troops arrived on the 25ᵗʰ May 1944. A large contingent was billeted in Cilfynydd, a small mining village to the north of Pontypridd. Once they were settled in they were called upon for details to assist other units as they arrived. They transported supplies and equipment to other areas.

A Unit History of the 94ᵗʰ tells the story under the title "Billeting Experiences in Wales," of the American view of their stay.

"Our relationships with the Welsh were excellent and we made many friends. The Welsh are interested in music and held many concerts to which members of the 94ᵗʰ were invited. They were welcome in their churches and clubs and became welcome guests to most activities.

On week-ends members of the 94ᵗʰ could draw their rations in kind to share with their hosts. Each officer and man could draw his piece of meat, a can of fruit and a can of vegetables instead of eating at the mess halls. These items were strictly rationed for the British and a welcome addition to their meagre store of food. We shared each other's food and enjoyed each other's company.

It was somewhat difficult for some to adjust to their overhead pull chains and shiny toilet paper. We marvelled at how much heat they could get out of their coal fireplaces with three lumps of coal the size of baseballs. The evenings were chilly and we sat in a semi-circle about the fireplace sipping tea, prepared in a kettle that sat on a stand near the heat of the fire. When it came to bedtime our host put a brick near the fire and gave it to the guest for warming the cold bed for the guest's feet. The sheets were flannel and most of us had bought flannel pajamas at the U.S.A. clothing store for the cold damp climate of Wales even in late spring and early summer.

Our experiences in Pontypridd were mostly all very favourable impressions. At first our personnel were not knowledgable of the strict rationing imposed on the British. A few days following the Battalion's arrival and billeting the C.O., Major William C. Burry, was visited by a local delegation of Pub Owners. They had a complaint that members of our unit had drunk their entire ration of beer and ale for the month in a couple of nights.

The C.O. sent some of his headquarters staff officers to the local rationing board and obtained a ration of kegs of beer and the 94th set up its own operation in the basement of a large building. This satisfied the local pub owners."

The Americans enjoyed the local social life and were very popular at the various dancehalls. Popular venues were the Star Ballroom in Mill Street and the Coronation Hall opposite St. Catherine's Church. Many officers were billeted in the Park Hotel and many parties held there. The Park Hotel was in Taff Street where Woolworths and the Midland Bank now stand.

The Pontpridd Observer gives examples of how the American forces played a part in local events.

Pontypridd Observer, Saturday April 4th 1944
A large congregation attended Carmel E.B. Church on Sunday evening when an American padre, Rev. E.B. Johnson occupied the pulpit. On the previous Sunday evening, Lieutenant Johnson was present at the evening service and accepted an invitation extended to him by the minister of the Church, Rev. B. David Johns, to preach at Carmel. During the course of the evening the Padre told all those present that he had found the hospitality of the people of Pontypridd to be of the highest order.

Soldiers from the 94th Medical Battalion outside the British Legion Hall in Pontypridd which was used as the Battalion Headquarters and Mess Hall. May 1944

William C. Burry was born in 1911 in Pittsburgh, Pennsylvania. He was educated at Pittsburgh State College and qualified as a Doctor in 1939. He received his appointment to the Regular Army Medical Corps on his Graduation Day. He was promoted to Commander of the 94th Medical Battalion in 1944.

1st Lt. Howard S. Doepke, the billeting officer for the 94th Medical Gas Treatment Battalion, recalls the events of 1944.

I was a member of the three person Advance Party of the 94th M.G.T.Bn. and arrived in Pontypridd directly from Kidderminster, England where we had requisitioned fifty-five vehicles for our battalion and carried on certain administrative duties. Beginning on May 18th 1944 it was my pleasure to accompany a member of the Pontypridd Police Department as we worked off a list of possible homes to billet our troops. When the main body of the 94th arrived in Pontypridd by troop train on May 25th 1944, all members were very surprised to learn that they would be guests of friendly Welsh families.

Being a school teacher prior to my entrance into the U.S.Army I found it most convenient to place myself with the headmaster of an elementary school in Pontypridd. My eleven weeks were made most enjoyable because of the kindness of Mr. and Mrs.Hayden Jones whose address was Preswylfer, Hawthorn, Pontypridd, Glamorgan. My stay with the Jones family was from May 18th until August 1st 1944 when our unit left for Normandy and became the Medical Holding Station for the U.S. Third Army.

My wife and I communicated with Mr. and Mrs. Jones until both passed away, they had always hoped to travel to the United States and never did so.

In my eleven weeks stay in Pontypridd (May, June, July) I must say I had little time to get much acquainted with my surroundings. I do have some most favourable memories of my time there. Here are a few of my recollections:

Going to church on a particular Sunday and being quite amazed at the quality and volume of the singing.

Our Battalion Headquarters being a bit off and above a city street with a large parking lot close by. I can't recall the exact location.

Standing in that same parking lot early on the morning of June 6th 1944 (D-Day) and looking into a sky almost black with Allied aircraft heading for Normandy.

Being invited by Hayden Jones (my host) to an evening affair at the school where he served as headmaster. The affair was a meeting of the mothers of the pupils who attended this school and it was the only time in my life that I was involved in a game of "Musical Chairs" which followed a lively meeting.

Seeing Hayden Jones heading off each evening on his Air Raid Warden watch dressed appropriately for the job. Bringing Madame Jones (my hostess) an orange from our army mess hall and noticing with surprise and pleasure that she used one piece of fruit to make a delicious cake.

1st Lt Howard S. Doepke

Battalion Headquarters
Rear:
CO S. Kimmelman, Cpt J. Torborg, Chap Cpt W. Soliday, !st Lt B. Beher, WOJG W. King
  Bn Motor O   Hq Det CO   Bn Chaplain   Supply O.   Personnel
Front:
1st Lt J. Kronz,   Major E. Irish,   LtC W. Burry,   Cpt V. Farrell,   1st Lt H. Deopk
  Adjutant   Executive Off   Bn Commanding O S-3 Operations   Evac O

Officers of A Company
Rear: Cpt Hassek, !st Lt Sibal, 1Lt Austin, 1st Lt Wempe, 1st Lt Kaplan, Cpt Bucholtz
Front: Cpt Bloom, Cpt Bleckman, Cpt Harry Q Fletcher, Cpt Brendel, Cpt Burn
Company Commander

The 94ᵗʰ Medical battalion in Pontypridd.

Officers of B Company
Rear: Cpt Camp, Cpt Buka, Cpt Lowenstein, Lt Bosveld, Lt Farr, Cpt Banner
Front: Cpt Balletto, Cpt ?, Cpt Greenham (CO), Cpt Lattermore, Cpt Hammell
Missing Cpt Krugar, D.C.

Officers of C Company Rear: Cpt Alex Gordon, Lt Hedlin, Cpt Nierbrief, Cpt Glanturko, Cpt
Letterese
Front: Cpt Joe Spanbock, Cpt Shaffer, Cpt John Carney (CO), Cpt Glutre,
Cpt Martin D.C.

Further extracts from the Unit History reveal more about the 94th Battalion's activities:

"To take up slack time the 94th drew some fifes and drums from the Quartermaster. There were a number of talented officers and men who practiced together as a 94th Fife and Drum Corps.

When they became proficient the 94th advertised and put on a Battalion parade complete with music and our Battalion colors. The Welsh enjoyed it. Most of the men who attended with their wives were World War 1 Veterans and they wore their medals on their lapels in honor of the occasion.

We had enjoyed our stay in "Ponty". We understood most of what they said when they spoke in English, but we did not know Welsh, which is a Gaelic language still taught in their schools and spoken among themselves at that time. The Welsh were a proud people who didn't care either for the English or the Scots which went a long way back in history."

Rhondda Leader Report July 8th 1944
Baseball Match. The baseball match which had to be postponed on Saturday will now take place on Thursday next at the Rugby Field, Ynysanghared Park at 6p.m. The game will be played by two teams of U.S. Forces and a novel feature will be that one team will consist of coloured players.

One of the GIs taking part in that match was James E. Anderson, now living in Fisher, Indiana in the U.S.A. He has kept a newspaper cutting of that event.

The 94th Medical battalion in Pontypridd.

Andy Anderson and two companions. Sgt. Andy Anderson on the right in the photograph

BASEBALL MATCH BROUGHT FORWARD

The baseball match which was postponed from July 1 until Thursday 13, took place last Saturday, 8 inst. The alteration was due to purely military reasons, and any inconvenience caused to anyone is deeply regretted. Owing to the very short notice of the change of date, the attendance was very much smaller than had been hoped. Two teams of U.S. forces took the field (one of which consisted of coloured players), and great interest was taken in the game by those present. However, a heavy downpour of rain caused the match to be abandoned after 30 minutes play. It is hoped to arrange another match shortly in aid of the Blind Institute, details of which will be given later. The winning numbers for the two ladies' shopping baskets were as follows: 2424 (orange ticket), 1292 (blue ticket). It is hoped that when a further match is arranged, the elements will be kinder both to spectators and the cause, namely, Pontypridd and District Institute for the Blind.

A BASEBALL MATCH was played on the Welfare Grounds on Saturday, and the proceeds were devoted to the Cilfynydd and Norton Bridge P.O.W. Funds. Two American teams battled with one another. Team 'A,' represented by Anderson, Schmidt, Cole, Todoro, Buckholtz, Power, Garrison, Kerrigan and Gabbett, beat Team 'B' (Rodregnez, Wiggand, Neel, Williams, Kuzniar, Leo, Sharboudy, Griffin, Cotton Crail, Cathbone, Lavally and Caldwell). Thanks are extended to the major-in-command Lt. Clements, and their colleagues for making the match possible and helping such worthy charities, while at the same time giving the spectators such a veritable treat.

Newspaper Cutting

A concert was held at Sardis Chapel in which American troops entertained a large audience. Involved in the items were Lt. John Torborg, Privates Cox, Smith, MacDonald and Mikels and Rev. Wayne Soliday (Chaplain).

The concert at Sardis Chapel is recalled by Chaplain (Colonel) Wayne E. Soliday:

The Rev. Gwyn Lewis was pastor of Sardis Chapel in Pontypridd. He asked me if I would line up some typical American music for a special "American Night" (Concert) in the Chapel. As with most Army troops we had a number of men from the Southern States. We were able to put together a rather representative group of musicians (honesty prompts me to add that not everyone who took part qualified as a "musician" but they did make their own unique contribution to the evening), that was July 16th 1944.

The event was well publicised: as a result the Chapel was filled to overflowing, so much so that there was only S.R.O.: that is Standing Room Only. Rev. Lewis introduced me (in a flowery and very flattering way) and indicated that I would preside. All went well and everyone appeared to be enjoying the evening. There was however, a thunderous out burst of laughter (at my expense) because of an embarrassing comment I made as I introduced the special soloist. His name (a fellow officer) will not be mentioned here, let me refer to him as Lieutenant "John Doe".

In order to explain the reason for the laughter I'll have to comment on the "relationships" enjoyed by some of the men and certain young Welsh girls. This relationship caused a number of problems as you might imagine. There were complaints by parents of these girls; there were some "knock down, drag out" confrontations involving soldiers and the young men of Pontypridd! I'll not go into detail as to the "goings on" between our men and the girls. However I believe I can explain my embarrassment as I prepared to introduce our special guest.

I intended to say, "It is now my privilege to present our special guest, Lt. John Doe, whose singing many of you have been enjoying". (I need to add that this officer had been singing at a number of special events in the civilian community, and was much in demand.) Instead of the above introduction I had planned, I found myself saying "It is now my privilege to present our special guest, whose LOVING MANY OF YOU HAVE BEEN ENJOYING...! Can you imagine my embarrassment?

The soloist and the Rev. Lewis (seated behind me), were the first to start laughing, followed immediately by all in attendance! After what seemed (to me) an eternity, quiet was resumed and I made the correct introduction...he sang an aria from an opera, at the end of which there was thunderous applause, and a call for "More...More...More."

I guess 'tis true: "All's well that ends well". Needless to say, as long as I live I'll remember that "goof" - and as long as the unit was together someone would remind me of that incident.

The warmth of the welcome the Americans received was recalled by Chaplain Soliday. He was billeted at 10 The Parade, Pontypridd, the home of the Reverend and Mrs. Gwyn Lewis.

We embarked from New York on the S.S.Uruguay on May 12th 1944 at 0930 hours. On May 24th we docked at Liverpool, England, around 1515 hours. The next morning we boarded a train at 1010 hours arriving in Pontypridd at 1700 hours.

I was accorded a very warm and comforting welcome by Gwyn and Edith Lewis and their only child Dawn (a charming little girl, I believe she was 6 or 7 years of age) added her words of welcome! During the time we were in Pontypridd (approximately 2-3 months) the Lewis family did everything to make my stay enjoyable.

I soon learned that such items as oranges and bananas were among the numerous food items (one other was coffee) that were in short supply in England. That discovery was made when I returned "home" one evening with an orange for Dawn. She seemed unusually pleased...her parents later told me until that incident she had never seen an orange. Thereafter, whenever fruit was available (and coffee) I would bring items home with me.

Another thing Dawn was pleased to receive was chewing gum; sometimes we would receive an issue of candy, mostly rolls of different flavoured hard candies. Before long I found there was a "welcoming committee" waiting for me as I approached the Parade. Dawn and her little friends had figured out about when "our American" (I found out she identified me in that way) would be arriving on the Parade! Pleasant memories.

When the war ended Chaplain Soliday returned to the United States and was released from the Army in February 1946 and served in two Baptist Churches in Hilltown and Allentown, Pennsylvania. On the morning of December 28th, 1950 he was recalled to active service and in August 1951 arrived in Korea. In later years he served as a U.S. Chaplain in Germany. He returned to America in 1964 and in 1966 was assigned as Staff Chaplain to the Military District of Washington.

Upon the death of General of the Army Dwight D. Eisenhower, the 34th President of the United States of America, on the 28th March 1969, Colonel Soliday was selected as the Military Chaplain, representing the U.S. Government during the State Funeral for General Eisenhower. The State Funeral took place on March 31st 1969 in Washington, D.C.

Chaplain (Colonel) Wayne E. Soliday

LAW AND ORDER

There was close and friendly co-operation between the local police and the American Authorities. The police were responsible for the billeting of the troops in private homes. The accompanied the soldiers in their trucks and jeeps as they negotiated the steep hills and awkward corners and narrow streets. Arriving at their billets the soldiers were introduced to their hosts.

Sgt. Moore based in Treorchy was typical of the local policemen. He was well known and a good friend to the American servicemen. He and the other regular policemen together with a large group of Specials saw that everything ran smoothly.

American troops were subject to American Army Law and if they committed any crime were dealt with by the American Army not the British legal system. An American Military Police Unit based in Porth supervised the behaviour of their servicemen and patrolled the streets in their jeeps wearing their distinctive white helmets.

A prison stockade was constructed on Llwyncelyn Field. Here black American soldiers awaiting trial for various crimes were detained. Prisoners were brought here from an area covering most of Glamorgan.

The American troops were very popular and their general behaviour was praised from many sources but everything was not always sweetness and light. Col. William C. Burry, Commander of the 94ᵗʰ Medical Battalion makes these comments in an article "Billeting Experiences in Wales".

"This was a mining town and there were many young miners exempt from military service because of their occupation. Our young men in uniform apparently competed with these young miners for the young ladies of Pontypridd. There were occasionally some altercations, a few bloody noses and shiners occasionally seen among members of the 94ᵗʰ, but no incident of complaint was ever forwarded to HQ by the Glamorgan Constabulary, which were our local civilian police. Our relationship with the police was excellent.

In response to a letter of appreciation to the local Constabulary for their kind assistance in getting our 94ᵗʰ billeted and helped in the re-supply and training, the Superindendent responded with the letter below reproduced and sent on our final day in Pontypridd."

Telephone № 2222

Glamorgan Constabulary.

Our Ref. W.P.71.
Your Ref. WCB/gh

" B "

Pontypridd.

31st July, 1944.

Division Office

All communications should be addressed to the Superintendent of Police.

Major William C. Burry
Officer Commanding,
U S. Forces,
Pontypridd.

Dear Major,

I should like to thank you for your letter of the 25th inst. and your kind remarks of appreciation.

I can assure you it has been a pleasure on the part of my men to assist your Organisation in any material way, and the high standard of co-operation reached was certainly a great credit to all concerned.

May I wish you and all those under your Command every success and Good Luck, in your coming operations.

Yours faithfully,

[signature]
SUPERINTENDENT.

LETTER – from local police to Colonel William C. Burry

Sgt. Moore (fourth from the left bottom row) played a major role in the billeting of American troops in the Treorchy area. He and the well known Estate Agent, John Thomas (extreme left top row) helped to organise the Cwmparc and Treorchy Welcoming Reception. John Thomas was Treasurer for the Welcoming Committee.

Glamorgan Special Constabulary – "G" Division – Treorchy Section, October22nd, 1944

From left to right back row
J. Thomas, G. Morris. ? , ? , ? , Jones, Reynolds, C. Higgon, A. Davies
Second row. Mr. Vaughan, D. Jones, O. Jones, ? ,Mr. Picton, A. Spiller, T. Eynon, ? ? Mr.
Hopkins, ? , Fred Vaughan
Third row. ? , E. Thomas, E. Davies, ? , W. Powell, ? ,I .Phillips, Mr. Reid, ?
F. George G Oram, T.D. Griffiths
Front Row. D. Edwards, R. Wood, D. Wood, Sgt. Moore, Insp. T. Jones, Insp. Evans, Insp. F.
Evans, M. Hughes, D. Davies, T. Jones, T. Davies

CHAPTER 14
The Departure

May 1944 was drawing to a close. It had been a dramatic month for the Rhondda. Over three thousand American troops had been billeted here and settled into family life with their hosts. There had been welcoming concerts in many of the main towns. The G.I.'s had settled into the social scene and had been made welcome in local churches, clubs and pubs. They frequented the local dance halls and cinemas and had been invited to numerous parties in individual homes. The Americans in turn had assisted in many charity events and had put on exhibition baseball games.

They had undergone their basic training in huge camps in the United States and then shipped to Britain. On arrival in carrying out their duties they had lived in various barracks and tented encampments. Now during May they had the unexpected but welcome experience of living in homes in the Rhondda where they had been made most welcome. They settled in quickly and enjoyed the family atmosphere. Pvt. Benjamin Gurdison from Baltimore, Maryland, and a member of the 186 Port Company based in Treherbert recalled "Most of the men were just considered part of the family by the people where they stayed. Hardly a night passed without having a chat over a cup of tea before retiring.

It was inevitable that this situation would not continue but when the order came to move out it was both sudden and dramatic.

Starting in the first week of May 1944 the soldiers and sailors of the Allied Expeditionary Force began descending on the ports of Southern England. They came by sea in a never ending stream of transports and landing craft. These ships came into every major port along the south coast of England and to ports along the Bristol Channel. To marshalling areas inland from these ports came troops and equipment by road and rail from Northern Ireland, Scotland, the Midlands and Wales.

It was about 9.00p.m.on May 30th that the order came for the troops of the 517 and 487 Port Battalions to make preparations to move out. All troops were ordered to report to their respective depots for further orders.

The suddenness of this dramatic news came as a shock to both the Americans and their hosts. The moment is recorded in the official records of the 186 Port Company, 487 Port Battalion.

"The 30th of May ended the Whitsun Bank Holiday of two days during which most of the men of the 186th Port Company had celebrated along with their Welsh hosts for it was also Decoration Day. Many recalled the last Decoration Day when the Battalion had proudly paraded through Brooklyn. Few thought what the morrow had in store.

It had rained in the late afternoon and the skies remained overcast. The night was pitch black as only a blacked out town set in a valley can be on a cloudy night. The stillness of the night was broken by the hurried footsteps of the C.Q. (the officer in charge of quartering) as he raced and stumbled all over Treherbert in search of several men needed in the Company orderly room immediately.

The next morning 31st May 1944 the Service Section left Treherbert and rode down the Valley through the towns, past cheering throngs who waved British and American flags. They too, knew that the Invasion was at hand.

The Service Section boarded a Liberty Ship, the Francis C. Harrington at Newport Docks. The three other platoons under Lts. Amis, Gensch and Spicuzza left Treherbert by truck for Pontypridd and then entrained for the marshalling area near Southampton.

Mrs. Verdun Lucas remembers such an event.

I remember what happened clearly. I was sitting in the second row in the upstairs circle with my daughter Marcia in the Empire Cinema in Tonypandy. The film stopped suddenly and a message was flashed on the screen that all American personnel were to report to their depots immediately. The hall lights went on and there were many American soldiers in the audience. They started to rush to the exits urged on by military police standing in the doorways. There was a general air of disquiet if not panic. Many of the girlfriends of the soldiers became very distressed and some became hysterical.

The cinema emptied with everyone leaving to find out what was happening. Stationary among the crowd milling about were large Army trucks with their engines running and further down the road, towards the railway station was a larger convoy of trucks. Some of the girlfriends were still creating a scene and clinging to the soldiers. I heard the military police shout "Enough of that" and ordered the

men into the trucks. Then crowded with soldiers they moved slowly until they were
clear of the throng, then picked up speed and were gone.

There was an unpleasant atmosphere, a feeling that something awful was going
to happen and you feared for the safety of those young soldiers."

The troops after reporting to their depots returned to their billets to pack their kit and personal belongings to be ready to leave in the morning. Some of the troops were not allowed to take any personal items or uniforms other than their combat outfits. These were to be collected later by military personnel. It was a time for hurried goodbyes and the writing of last notes, letters home and personal messages to friends male and female.

In many homes where the troops had lived as part of the family, there were many sad farewells and a few tears shed. At 6am on May 31st, they reported to their assembly points.

In hundreds of homes the departure of the Americans had their own individual stories.

Mr. Edgar Powell lived at 1 Station Road, Penygraig and his parents had one G.I. staying with them. On the morning of May 31st the American thanked them for the kindness they had shown him and gave them a parcel for safe keeping. He asked that if anything were to happen to him would they be willing to deliver it together with a letter to his girlfriend in Whitchurch, Cardiff. He then joined the other soldiers from the area as they formed up on the green in front of St. Barnabas Church. They then boarded waiting U.S. Army trucks and were gone.

Sadly, the trip to Whitchurch had to be made.

Mrs. Muriel Williams remembers the American departure from Ferndale. It was a very sad affair. In the homes where they had been staying everyone was upset. It was not just that they were leaving but the reason for their departure and the fear that some of them were going to get killed overshadowed everything. The trucks were lined up in Maxwell Street and the soldiers climbed in with their equipment. As the trucks moved off and everyone waved goodbye all the women and girls were crying and many of the men were visibly upset.

This picture was repeated along the length of both Rhondda Valleys. As each Company joined the convoy, so it increased in length until there was one long line of slow moving trucks stretching out of sight. The trucks from both valleys converged at Porth and there were many holdups.

The convoy moved slowly to Pontypridd, the town was at a standstill with every street and road full of backed up lorries.

In their slow progress down the Valleys the pavements were lined with crowds of people waving and calling out and many in tears. It was like a scene from a film one witness recalled.

Over a thousand troops from the 487 Port Battalion entrained at Pontypridd railway station on their way to the marshalling areas around Southampton. The 517 Port Battalion continued by road to the South Wales ports. The traffic jam eventually cleared and the last truck left to waves from the crowd.

The 517 and 487 Port Battalions were on their way to the beaches of Normandy and the fateful events of the 6th of June, D-Day.

Bill Churchill 1944
Bill Churchill in 1944. He was employed as a driver by the Ministry of Supply to transport ammunition and explosives from Bridgend Arsenal to military bases in other areas of Britain. He witnessed the huge American convoys travelling to the Invasion ports.

Bill Churchill of Penygraig encountered the huge convoys heading for the Channel ports. He was employed as a driver by the Ministry of Supply. His job involved transporting explosives and munitions from the Royal Ordnance Factory in Bridgend to the various arsenals in the country. On June 1st 1944 he was returning from the Woolwich Arsenal in London when he met up with this great movement of military vehicles as he approached the Cotswolds. Military traffic had priority and there were many delays for civilian lorries.

Mr. Churchill recalls, "I was forced to park on the side of the road many times to let this military traffic pass. There were trucks loaded with troops and equipment, jeeps, ambulances, weapons carriers, huge Diamond T breakdown trucks and giant tank transporters conveying tanks by the hundreds. It was an unbelievable sight and one nobody would ever witness on such a scale again. From the area of the Cotswolds into South Wales was one unbroken column of military vehicles."

When the troops arrived in their marshalling areas they made up an army of two million men and nearly half a million vehicles. They were all centred on the ports of Plymouth, Torquay, Weymouth, Bournemouth, Southampton, Portsmouth, Eastbourne and others along the southern coastline. The Bristol Channel ports of Bristol, Newport, Cardiff, Barry, Penarth and Swansea were used to embark troops to be used in the follow up phase of the Invasion.

The 487 Port Battalion moved down to the area near the port of Southampton. The 517 Port Battalion moved to marshalling areas near Barry and Singleton Park, Swansea. Both took part in the D-Day landings on Omaha Beach.

The 94th Medical Battalion remained in the Pontypridd area until the 31st of July when it received orders to move to the coastal marshalling area near Romsey. They arrived on August 2nd and were loaded in combat formation in Portsmouth and shipped across to Normandy.

The American presence in the Rhondda had ended, a brief but unique chapter in the story of the Rhondda had come to a close.

A NURSE'S STORY

In 1944 Elsie Wescombe was a member of the Civil Nurses Reserve. Although a qualified nurse she was not employed in that capacity because she had got married a year earlier. Nurses together with teachers had to give up their jobs if they married under the rules in force in the Rhondda.

However because of the demands that the war was making on the available workforce things were forced to change. In 1943 national service was compulsory for single women between the ages of nineteen and twenty-four. From February 1942 married women aged between twenty and thirty could only be employed through Government Employment Exchanges which ensured their direction into essential war industries.

The demand for nurses was so great that Elsie Wescombe was conscripted into the nursing service and based at Porth Hospital.

When the American troops arrived one G.I. named George Lepkanich of the 798th Port Company, 517 Port Battalion was billeted in the Wescombe's family home at 54 Charles Street, Porth. He was accepted as one of the family and was a constant companion with Elsie's father when they set off to the Wyndham Club.

As D-Day approached large scale preparations were made for the treatment of wounded troops. Many of the staff at Porth Hospital were put on reserve for Whitchurch Hospital which had been cleared to accept the expected wounded.

On June 1st 1944 the American troops moved out of the Rhondda for the Normandy invasion. In less than a week in fact five days later some of these same troops were being brought back as casualties and some would never return.

The wounded were landed in the southern ports in England and transported on hospital trains to a special halt constructed at Whitchurch. They were then brought in convoys of ambulances to the hospital. Assisting in this movement of the wounded was the U.S. 94th Medical Battalion based at Pontypridd. The wounded on the 6th and 7th of June were brought straight off the beaches and arrived at Whitchurch Hospital still with only field dressings.

Rhydlafar had been built as an American Hospital but in the days immediately following the Invasion all Allied troops were brought to Whitchurch which had a capacity of 1,500 beds.

Nurse Wescombe worked in the surgical ward dealing with amputations and severe head wounds. She said that the introduction and use for the first time of the wonder drug penicillin undoubtedly saved many lives.

Nurse Elsie Wescombe in 1944

In anticipation of heavy casualties from the D-Day Invasion and subsequent campaigns extensive preparations were made by the Hospital Authorities to cope with the expected influx of wounded soldiers.

Church Village Hospital was opened in 1937 and gradually it had been extended and enlarged. Serious delays occurred because of the shortage of concrete, priority had been given to the construction of runways at the airbases of the Allied Air Forces. It developed as a major centre for the treatment of British and Canadian wounded aircrew.

Rhydlafar Hospital was financed and built by the Americans in 1943. Known as the 348 (U.S.) Station Hospital it dealt solely with American casualties and employed American and British nurses.

Whitchurch Hospital was cleared of all civilian patients who were moved to general hospitals in the surrounding areas. Nurses were drafted in from the Rhondda and elsewhere some weeks before the Invasion. On D-Day itself and for several days later wounded soldiers from Normandy were brought straight from the battlefield still wearing their field dressings. A large number of American and British wounded were brought there. Unloaded at various docks they were brought by hospital trains to a special halt constructed at Whitchurch.

With the transfer of many nurses to these military hospitals and also the influx of patients from these same hospitals meant local hospitals were seriously understaffed. The problem was solved by the use of trained nurses and nursing auxillaries from detachments of the Red Cross.

One of the Red Cross Detachments was based in Treorchy.

Treorchy Red Cross 1944
The man seated centre front row is Dr. Fergus Armstrong a well known local surgeon and doctor.
The lady to his right is Dr. Ackerman a partner in his medical practice.

The American Army leaves the Rhondda Date 1ˢᵗ June 1944. Place: approaching Pontypridd.
Destination: Omaha Beach.

Extract from the Memoirs of Pfc. Arthur F. Bonner

After several months we were shipped to Wales where we were given some practice in beach unloading and we were billeted in private homes, two American soldiers to each home. As the Army trucks rolled down the streets, they stopped at homes that had agreed to accept soldiers and two were assigned as we went along.

The name of the little town was Treorchy in the Rhondda Valley. So Wales and I had the good fortune to live with the Exell Family (Mr. & Mrs. Colin Exell and their four children). Their younger son, Gordon and I became very good friends which resulted in a lifetime friendship of over 45 years. Living standards in Treorchy were about twenty-five years behind ours and an interesting experience for an American lad. The bathroom was in the backyard and the bathtub (per se) was a copper tub in the basement that had to be filled from hot water from the stove before we bathed. We were accepted and treated like family and they enjoyed fussing over us.

Mr. Exell was a coal miner and the town was in a valley surrounded by mountains. Very often Gordon and I climbed to the top of one of the mountains where we practiced target shooting. It was a great thrill for Gordon (who was 18 years old) to use an American carbine. The family was on war rations so we G.I.s would often sneak home extra Army rations. It was a most pleasant place to be prior to the invasion of Europe which we knew was not too far off.

In June 1944 about four days before the invasion, we were spirited down to Southampton before boarding merchant ships. We were told we would leave on the 5th of June for France. However the weather being intolerable, General Eisenhower delayed the invasion one day until the 6th of June.

On the day before the actual invasion we were aboard a small freighter that had once been used against the invasion in Italy which was carrying 50,000 five gallon cans of gasoline and medical supplies. The night of June 5th we sat on board playing cards and tried to imagine what would happen next day. Sometime near midnight we were informed we would have to wait another day since the weather was intolerable for an invasion and maybe the next day would be better. On the 6th of June at midnight orders came through that we were to head for France our destination was given to us at that time we were to land at Dog Red Beach on Omaha. Not many of us slept that night.

V-MAIL

The regular supply of mail from America to the U.S. soldiers in Europe was regarded by the U.S. Government as essential to their morale. There were over a million and a half American personnel and the logistic problems of moving the tens of thousands of sacks of mail to and from the States were immense. Mail communications from the States to all overseas points were enhanced by the V-mail. Free preprinted sheets were provided to the troops and their friends and relatives back home. Written on one page, the sheets were then microfilmed and sent by air to their destination area and the film was then printed to one third of its original size. Delivery to European sites took about five days. A tremendous development for morale all round. Below is an example of a V-mail sent by Pfc. Arthur Bonner from his billet in Treorchy back to his home in the United States.

V-Mail

The use of a magnifying glass was recommended. Prior to this invention mail arrived by ship and could take many weeks to arrive and be distributed. It also took up valuable space on the ships bringing in vital war supplies. An example of this is shown in the Monthly Training Report of the 517 Port Battalion from 1st January to 25th January 1944. 13,248 tons of cargo discharged. Approximately 15,000 bags of U.S. mail loaded and discharged.

The Rhondda and U.S. Soldiers Copy of an article in the New York Tribune by Roma Saunders.

Western Mail June 27th 1944

America Your Boys are Loved in Wales

There are many lonely homes in South Wales. Reason is that Americans they grown to regard as members of their families have left for the Second Front.

The Welsh hosts were as sorry to see them go as if they were their own sons. They are waiting eagerly to hear from them to know how they are faring in the battle. They hope that some day they will be able to welcome them "home" again to meet the youngsters who are sharing in this fight for democracy.

In their own inimitable way these men and women from across the Atlantic have cemented Anglo-American friendship.

In a tour of the area in which they had been billeted I discovered one thing. When householders were told many months ago that they were to have American soldiers billeted on them they did not want them. Our lads are in the fight they argued. Our daughters have had to go away from home to do war work. Why should we put up with Americans? Why can't they be put in camps?

They were in fact about as popular as evacuees had been in the early part of the war.

Not Tough Guys

Like the evacuees however the Americans soon found their seat at the Welsh fireside. The housewife who expected difficulties about meals, beds and hours found she had nothing to worry about except in a few isolated cases.

As for the man in the house he found a new interesting companion. The yarns he had spun so often to the family were eagerly received by his American boarder. They swapped yarns over tea and ale.

In a much shorter time than it takes an official to cut red tape these ordinary men of Wales and America had got to know one another, their likes and dislikes, how they differed from each other; better still how they could overcome these difficulties.

Welsh hosts took their guests to the pictures. They went home to point out how different film life was from the normal American or British life.

Take Mrs. A. Jones of Princess Street Pontypridd for instance. She found her two Chicago soldiers were anything but "tough guys" as depicted in the American gangster films. In spite of their 6ft and corresponding breadth they were "grand boys" Mrs. Jones said, "You could not wish for two nicer fellows".

Then there is Mrs. C.F. Llewellyn also of Princess Street. Two Americans one from Virginia and the other from New York billeted on her thought Pontypridd one of the prettiest places they had seen and repeatedly told her if they were not so far from home they would like to stay there.

Wept a Bit

Throughout the Rhondda Valley the Doughboys won the hearts of their hosts and hostesses. The miner thought they were lads after his own heart. They loved the freedom.

They wanted to work and spent their leisure hours with their families in the evenings. They lent a hand with the allotment, went to chapel with the family on Sunday, played ball with young Johnie, kicked a ball around in the local football field, taught the Welsh lads how to play baseball. In return the Americans learnt to appreciate rugby.

They exchanged "snaps" and many American soldiers and nurses are now standing on French soil with photographs to remind them of their Welsh friends they left behind when the call came to take part in the Invasion of Europe.

I called at terrace houses and saw photographs of these young Americans standing side by side with Welsh uniformed men and women on the piano they had so often gathered round for that Sunday evening sing-song. The photographs were just as proudly displayed in the detached homes of solicitors and other professional men. Some day the wife of a solicitor told me we hope to see "our boy" again. He was just like one of the family.

"We haven't a son of our own and when he came I tried to put myself in his mother's place. I must confess I wept a bit when he left us."

No America, Wales will not forget your young men and women. A number of American Army nurses were billeted in the Whitchurch area of Cardiff and received the same homely welcome as the soldiers in the Rhondda. They too were held in high regard by their hosts. They were proud to know them. Some day they hope to accept the invitation your parents sent them to visit you in your home towns. They'll be glad to know the parents and wives, brothers and sisters of the ambassadors you sent over here in this Second European War.

CHAPTER 15

The Invasion and Campaigns in Europe

THE 487 PORT BATTALION

The 487 Port Battalion was part of the United States First Army and had been assigned to the 5th Engineer Special Brigade.

It was to form part of the assault force to land on Omaha Beach on D-Day.

The troops moved from their permanent station in the Rhondda on June 1st 1944 to marshalling areas and were loaded on coasters at Newport and Southampton on the 5th and 6th of June. Departure from Southampton was delayed by naval orders to the various shipmasters and on D-Day 6th June the originally planned units arrived off Omaha after a fairly uneventful crossing of the English Channel.

Included in the photograph are Pvt. William J Ferrell, Tec.5 Taylor J Plaisance, Tec.5 Clifford S Linstead, Sgt. George W Nic, T. Sgt. Michael J Menchise, Cpl. Edward B Schular and Cpl. Albert F Froment. All had been billeted in Treherbert

The assault on the Omaha Beach had been planned to the last detail but most things that could go wrong did and the beach became known as "Bloody Omaha" with good reason. The air strike that was intended to eliminate the German defensive positions before the Americans came ashore missed the target and left the German defences largely unscathed. The impressive rocket bombardment was also ineffective. The landing craft and amphibious tanks came under withering fire and the 1st Infantry Division could not get off the beach. They and the Engineer Special Brigades suffered severe casualties.

Sunrise D-Day June 6th 1944

View of Omaha Beach from coaster

Upon arrival on D-Day the coasters carrying the 487 Port Battalion came in close to the shore to discharge supplies for the assault troops but because of the chaos few DUKWs or other ferry craft came alongside. The coasters loaded with petrol and ammunition were ordered further out and moved accordingly. Only a few coasters managed to get supplies ashore under extremely dangerous circumstances. All were being subject to hostile artillery and sporadic air attack.

On the morning of D-Day +1 Headquarters Staff got ashore and DUKWs began to go out to the ships for much needed ammunition

151

Omaha Beach. On the morning of D-Day + 1 the Port Headquarters staff got ashore and DUKW's began to go to the ships for much needed ammunition and fuel and unloading from ship to shore

The debris of war, humans and material litter the beach.
The clear-up begins although still under air attack.

The Port Comapnies get the vital materials ashore. Note the French children risking life and limb to get candy and gum.

A group of G.I.s take a break from training on the mountains above Treherbert, Rhondda, Wales. The same group, a week later, Omaha Beach, Normandy, France.

Once the beach-head had been secured then men and material poured ashore. The 487 Port Battalion played a vital role in unloading material directly on to the beach and by utilising the Mulberry Harbour at St. Laurent-Sur-Mer. The great storm of June 9th badly damaged this harbour and it was abandoned. The 487 Port Battalion worked in this area until October 10th 1944 when it was moved to the famous floating harbour at Arromanches.

When the Allies captured Antwerp the Battalion received orders to move to the Port of Antwerp. It left Arromanches on November 8th 1944 and moved to Lison, France where a train of "forty and eight" box cars were to take them on the long journey to Antwerp, Belgium. After travelling for four days and three nights they arrived in the railway yard in Antwerp to be greeted by their first Buzz-Bomb.

Mud

487 Port Battalion Official Report – Omaha Beach
With the cessation of enemy resistance and comparative stabilization of operations, the battalion moved from enemy trenches and hastily built foxholes on the beach to a spacious and sanitary bivouac area where every possible improvement was introduced for insuring the continued health, comfort and morale of the troops.

Camp Buhot was established on the flat plain overlooking Arromanches. Everywhere there was mud. Pfc. Leon Miller recalled

"The men were used to mud from Omaha Beach. But here it was different, there was no way of avoiding walking in at least four inches of it. Pvt. William Duffy, from the same 186 Port Company, description is, "Everywhere we go its nothing but mud, mud, mud. When we ate, when we work, when we go to town and even when we go to sleep. Some of the tents have floors but ours didn't, it was dear old mother earth in liquid form. Occasionally when we get a chance to work on the ships by the end of the day our shoes have dried and the mud fallen off. Back in camp it was still waiting for us. We used to hear stories about mud from the last war, but never has it been so realistic."

The 487 and 517 Port Battalions were transported from France to the Port of Antwerp by means of "forty and eight" boxcars. The journey took four days and three nights to complete. The "forty and eight" designation meant that the boxcars could carry forty men or eight horses.

Luchtbal Barracks their "hoem" for the next seven months until the end of the war.

1ˢᵗ Sgt. Wilbert J. Schuman and Sgt. Joseph F. Lutz 186 Port Company, 487 Port Battalion, U.S. Army.

During the Second World War the photographing of any military activity was a criminal offence and would result in imprisonment for any British civilian. However many American servicemen had cameras and were also able to obtain films from the PX stores.

Sgt. Schuman was a keen photographer and took hundreds of photographs recording the history of the 487 Port Battalion. It is thanks to him that a visual record exists of the presence of the 487 Port Battalion in the Rhondda.

His enthusiasm and skill is illustrated in his photograph of a Vl-Rocket hurtling down on his barracks in Antwerp with him placed dangerously close to the point of impact.

Several members of his Battalion were killed and injured by this bomb.

Buzz Bomb

Damage to garage Luchtbal Barracks, Antwerp, Belgium

They were housed in Luchtbal Barracks in the northern part of Antwerp close to the docks. The Battalion worked in these docks under constant attack from V-1 and V-2 Rockets. These missiles dropped continuously night and day for four months. Some 50 to 70 landed every day. They remained operating the docks until the end of the war. They then moved to Ghent in Belgium and finally to Bremerhaven in Germany.

The vital importance of Antwerp to the Allies in their campaign in North-West Europe is illustrated by these two photographs taken by a member of the 487 Port Battalion.

BROWN NOSE

Recruited in England in its capacity as company mascot it accompanied the 186 Port Company to Treherbert. It left with the 487 Port Battalion for the D-Day Invasion.

An account of its military activity on D-Day is recorded in the Company's official history by Tec.5 Lawrence Silverman.

"When it rains it pours and very often it isn't iodised table salt or rain. Lt. Amis platoon had more than their share of troubles. It seemed that the Germans had their 88s zeroed in on the "Rocklease", nor did the fact that their cargo was "hot stuff" (400 tons of ammunition) make the men any happier. In some manner the ship rammed a breakwater caisson which was to have been part of the artificial port planned for the beach. The coaster then pushed against another ship and almost lost its mast. Brown Nose, Bill Duffy's pet mongrel almost lost a tonsil barking at the other ship.

On November 8th the Company moved from Arromanches to Lison where they boarded a train of forty and eight boxcars to take them on the long journey to Antwerp. Sgt. Tom McCarthy records what happened to Brown Nose.

Enroute to Antwerp the train made several stops and at some of these stops things happened that will go down in the mind. Pvt's Kossa and Buchera saw a small baker's shop about a hundred yards from the train and decided they would get a few loaves of French bread. While in the shop our train gave the signal to move on and we left two men to go down as A.W.O.L.s. Another instance, Pvt. Jack Mantock was looking for a latrine and after a long hunt found one. He was sitting comfortably when three blasts from the engine signalled we were off again so a third man went missing.

Last but not least in A.W.O.L.s was our small dog Brown Nose, the Company mascot. He had joined us in England and the whole Company had taken a liking to him. He disappeared at one of our many stops and that was the last we saw of the little shaver."

Brown Nose
Company Mascot of the 186 Port Company

May 8th 1945 was declared Victory in Europe Day by General Eisenhower and to the entire world meant the end of a long and arduous campaign. A celebration parade was held in Antwerp on May 9th in which British, American, French and Polish troops took part.

This photograph shows the 487 Port Battalion on parade. These were the soldiers who had been billeted in the Rhondda Fawr in an area extending from Tonypandy to Treherbert.

Victory Parade

THE 517 PORT BATTALION

The 517 Port Battalion was assigned to the United States First Army and formed part of the 6th Engineer Special Brigade.

It would join the assault on Omaha Beach on D-Day. On June 1st 1944 it moved out of the Rhondda to the marshalling areas at Barry and Singleton Park, Swansea.

There they boarded coasters and sailed to the assembly areas off the coast of Normandy. On June 6th specially trained companies of the 517 Port Battalion together with other units of the 6th Engineer Special Brigade landed on Omaha Beach. These special beach demolition teams suffered heavy casualties. The remainder of the Battalion landed on Omaha Beach on June 8th.

Once the beach was secure the Battalion commenced its duties Cargo unloaded directly on the beach. By June 10th they were operating from Vierville-Sur-Mer. By August they had moved along the coast to St. Laurent-Sur-Mer. Their duties remained the unloading of cargo on the Omaha Beach.

On Nov. 24th 1944 the 517 Port Battalion travelled by train to the Port of Antwerp. They were transported by "forty and eight" box cars and they arrived at the railway yard in Antwerp on Nov. 29th. Their duty at the Port of Antwerp was the discharging cargo from ships and checking the unloading onto trucks, trains, barges and the storage of all types of cargo discharged.

Antwerp being a vital port for the Allies came under heavy attack from the Germans. For one hundred and seventy five days the Port of Antwerp came under continuous air and V-weapon attack.

They were housed in Luchtbal Barracks where they joined the 487 Port Battalion.

The 517 Medical Detachment when in the Rhondda had a medical dispensary and first aid post in the basement of the New York Hotel in Porth. Dodge army ambulances were stationed outside. Seriously ill patients had been taken to the 384th. U.S. Station hospital at Rhydlafar.

Now in Antwerp the men of the Detachment were on call constantly to aid in rescue work in various parts of the city. The greatest catastrophe to befall the Battalion and in which the Medical Detachment did great work was in a V-bombing of a theatre in Antwerp, the "Rex Theatre". The Battalion lost fourteen dead and a greater number in wounded men.

The Detachment was dispatched to the scene of the incident and carried on rescue work all day and through the night, doing yeomen work. There were other occasions when the Detachment was called upon to do rescue work, but this was the greatest.

On the 4th of September 1945 each man of the 517th Medical Detachment received a certificate from the people of the City of Antwerp in appreciation of and as a token of gratitude for his work in the Port of Antwerp during the air attacks.

The 517 Port Battalion was still in Antwerp when the war ended in May 1945.

THE BATTLE FOR ANTWERP

In September 1944 the British Army liberated Antwerp, Belgium. They had the seaport facilities operational two months later to supply the British, American, Canadian and French forces fighting in Europe. Antwerp became a vital factor in the final months of the Second World War. In desperation, the Germans made the city a top priority target for their infamous V-Weapons.

The V-Weapons were also known as the V-1 Flying Bomb or Buzz Bomb and the V-2 Rocket. They were short-range missiles and were fired at Antwerp from launch sites in German occupied Netherlands and Western Germany. Almost 5,000 Flying Bombs were launched in a frantic 154-day effort by Hitler to demolish the port that was to mean his end.

This was foiled by Antwerp X. This super secret operation involving 22,000 anti-aircraft gunners using the finest artillery guns was commanded by the American Brig.-General Clare H. Armstrong. It was a mixed force of British, American and Polish troops. They shot down thousands of the V-1 Buzz Bombs. There was no defence against the V-2 Rockets.

The troops of the 487 and 517 Port Battalions, who had been billeted in the Rhondda, carried on with their vital work of unloading supplies throughout this bombardment.

On the 16th December 1944 at 3.30 in the afternoon a V-2 Rocket scored a direct hit on the Rex Theatre in Antwerp. It was crowded with off-duty soldiers and civilians and 567 people were killed and 291 injured. Among those casualties were 296 soldiers killed and 193 soldiers injured and these included troops from the 487 and 517 Port Battalions. In fact for the 517 Port Battalion it was their highest casualty loss suffered in one day with the loss of 14 dead and a much higher number wounded.

The 517 Medical Detachment did heroic work over the two day rescue and was awarded formal recognition for their bravery and dedication to duty by the City of Antwerp.

Rex Theatre, Antwerp
The Rex Theatre destroyed by a V-2 Rocket 16th Decmeber1944
The V-Weapons on display in Antwerp in 1945. Photographs taken by members
of the 487 Port Battalion.

The V-1 Flying Bomb

V2 Rocket

THE FINAL PARADE

The final chapter in the wartime story of the 487 and 517 Port Battalions was drawing to a close. A final parade was held in Antwerp for the presentation of the Purple Heart to wounded soldiers from both Battalions.

They had spent the major part of their stay in Britain in South Wales. The 517 Port Battalion arrived at Hayes Lane Camp in Barry in September 1943 and had then been deployed in the docks in Barry and Cardiff. The 487 Port Battalion had arrived in Newport on January 5th 1944.

After being assigned to Engineer Special Brigades and undergoing amphibious training both Battalions were moved to the Rhondda. It was in the Rhondda that the special relationship developed with the Welsh. In the people's homes they enjoyed the hospitality for which the Rhondda was famous. A special bond grew up between many of the servicemen and their hosts which lasted over many years.

Now, after experiencing the grim conditions of the war in North-West Europe those who had survived were going home.

The initial preparations are under way, the presentation group stand ready to undertake the award ceremony. Luchtbal Barracks form an austere backdrop to the photograph.

Presentation Group

Troops presentation

These photographs show a panoramic view of the troops formed up for the medal presentation. The Schelt Estuary and Antwerp Docks can be viewed in the background.

Purple Heart Presentation

The Purple Heart is presented to members of the 517 Port Battalion. They stand proudly accompanied by an Honour Guard bearing the stars and stripes and the Battalion and Transportation Corps flags.

HEADQUARTERS
517TH PORT BN, TC
APO 562 U S ARMY

24 October 1945

SUBJECT: Port Battalion Activities

TO: Chief of Transport,
United States service Forces,
European Theater,
APO 887 US Army,
(Thru Channels)

1. The pictorial Handbook of Military Transportation, prepared by the Transportation corps, ETO, has just been received and reviewed with eager anticipation, much interest and keen disappointment.

2. Once more, continuing the record which stands unblemished and unbroken to date, your soldier stevedores and their work remain anonymous, unhonored and unsung.

3. As one leafs through this otherwise excellent pictorial saga one finds well deserved credit given to TC s GI trainmen, drivers, shopmen, divers builders, repairmen and others but what of the GI stevedore? One finds well earned recognition of the dukw companies, railroad shop, construction and operating battalions, truck companies, harbor craft companies, marine maintenance companies, Major Ports and hospitals, - but what of the Port Battalions and Port Companies?

4. All but the merest drop of the vast flood of supplies and material poured onto this continent has been carried in ships. Every agency and half a hundred facilities have been available to bring that cargo to, and to dispatch it from, the shipside, but every bit of it has been handled by the stevedores. And from June the 6,1944 until the Port of Antwerp was opened in December, that first two million tons put ashore over the beaches of Omaha and Utah, through the ports of Aromanches, Cherbourg, La Havre and Rouen was handled entirely by our own GI stevedores under conditions that engraved every word of the monotony, sweat, toil and death of War, in capital letters.

5. There is a real disappointment in the hearts of many thousands of soldier stevedores that their part in TC activities has been so consistently disregarded and unrecognized.

HAROLD E BONAR
Lt. Colonel, TC
Commanding

Letter from Harold Bonah

THE 94th MEDICAL BATTALION

The 94th Medical Battalion moved out of Pontypridd on August 1st 1944. Their trucks, jeeps and ambulances made the long journey across country to Romsey in Hampshire their marshalling area. They arrived on August 2nd and were loaded in combat formation in Portsmouth and shipped across to Normandy.

They had been assigned to the U.S. Third Army under the command of Lieut- General George S. Patton. As the Third Army fought its campaigns in France and then on to Germany the 94th Medical Battalion followed in a combat support operation.

Their first site was at Gael which was a trial run using only Company B. All the remainder of the sites as they advanced East were operated by the entire 94th. In many cases there was an overlap of dates as some elements began operating in the newer locations while those remaining behind were utilised until all evacuees were flown out. This leapfrog operation proved to be an asset to a unit with three similar Companies A, B and C.

Short stays of one or two week duration occurred at Beile, St.Peravy La Columbe, Vertus and Etain. The 94th was then at Toul from the 21st September to the 30th of November 1944. It was the region's rainy season and they had to cope with appalling muddy conditions. From there they moved to Thionville and a lengthy stay from the 1st of December 1944 to March 4th 1945. It was here that the Battalion was assembled in Battle Formation to receive the Meritorious Service Award, the first to be awarded in the entire Third United States Army.

While at Thionville the 94th dealt with the casualties from the Battle of the Bulge. The Third Army under the leadership of General Patton changed direction to the north-east of Thionville to strike at the German forces besieging Bastogne.

The campaign to save St. Vith and Bastogne began on December 19th 1944 and ended on the 28th of January 1945. When Bastogne was completely opened up stretcher cases were brought to the 94th for evacuation. The campaign cost the U.S. Army 50,630 casualties and those who were not killed were evacuated by the Battalion.

When the American Army pushed into Germany the 94th followed. They were based in Rothenbergen, Germany from the 3rd to the 12th of April and dealt with large numbers of repatriated prisoners of war. When the Third Army overran German defences there were thousands of captured Allies who were medically checked, deloused, showered, clothed and loaded onto military cargo planes for repatriation to England, France and Belgium.

The 94th now moved on to Gotha further to the east of Germany. They had just established camp along the runway of a former German bomber station when they were surprised to see three light aircraft land with three high ranking military men. They were General Omar Bradley of 12th Army Group, General George Patton Commander of the Third U.S. Army and the Supreme Allied Commander General Eisenhower.

The reason for such a high ranking visit was soon revealed. An hour's drive from Gotha was a place called Buchenwald the site of the notorious concentration camp. The military leaders had come to see the horrors of the camp at first hand.

From Gotha the Battalion continued its eastern progress crossing the River Danube and arrived in Regensberg which was to be its last operational base.

In eleven months of operational support of combat operations the 94th evacuated over 90,000 personnel by rail, air and motor vehicles. These were a miscellaneous group of U.S., Allied and German wounded. It was the command and co-ordinating nucleus for a variety of field army units, Field Hospitals, clearing units, ambulance companies, litter bearers and collecting.

During a span of little over 29 months between May 1943 and September 1945 it was activated, trained and shipped to Britain. It participated in the Invasion and combat support until the end of the European war. It was quickly returned to the U.S.A. sailing from Cherbourg on July 20th 1945. The Battalion was returned for rest and rehabilitation with plans to ship it to the Pacific. Peace came and it was de-activated shortly thereafter.

(These facts are derived from the official unit history of the 94th Battalion produced by Col. William C. Burry)

WITH THE 94th MEDICAL BATTALION IN EUROPE

TOUL-FRANCE A muddy airstrip   *The 4-wheel drive was needed*

TOUL railway station. The first hospital train   *Ambulances load wounded into a waiting C-47*

Crossing the Rhine on pontoon brifges

Crossing the German border Captains Carney and Neidric

Ambulances evacuating 94th en route to Air Strip Germany

Approaching the Danube River crossing, Germany 1945

Lt-Col Burry and his jeep in the Nazi Amphitheatre at Nuremburg, Germany.

Captain Werner Lowenstein

Captain Lowenstein was a doctor serving with the 94th Medical Battalion. He emigrated from Germany to the United States in 1937. He had graduated from medical school in Germany in the last year that Jews were permitted to graduate from professional schools.

After going through internship again in the United States and becoming a licensed doctor and a U.S. citizen, he joined the Army. As a member of the 94th Medical Battalion he found himself back in Germany, treating wounded soldiers, German as well as American. He was among the U.S. troops who liberated Buchenwald concentration camp.

"When my father encountered a wounded S.S. officer who needed blood, my father would say to him, "Wir haben nur Blut von Schwartzen oder Juden"; (We have blood only from Blacks and Jews).

Those of you who are aware of the centrality of Hitler's purity myths in the Nazi regime will appreciate the irony of the unanimous response of those S.S. in need; "Das macht nichts". (It doesn't matter) Blood is blood after all, and its common denominator is always red, despite the race of the donor.

There isn't much humour to be found in the Holocaust. Perhaps this is it; a Jewish doctor telling wounded S.S. officers they are about to receive blood from Untermenschen.

Miriam Zimmerman writes for the National Jewish Post and Opinion in the U.S.A.

CHAPTER 16

Postscript

In looking back to the events of 1944 it is remarkable that over half a century later the former American servicemen still hold the Rhondda and the Welsh people in such high regard.

Among the local Rhondda people the American presence in those unique and historic times still evokes many vivid and pleasant memories.

Of all the recollections of their stay it is the suddenness of their departure is the one most commented upon.

"One minute they were here, the next they were gone."

Many of the G.I.s kept in contact with their former hosts for many years after the war. A number of them took advantage of short periods of leave to make the long journey back to the Rhondda from Europe despite the difficulties and delays of wartime travel. Some in later years spent holidays here renewing past friendships. As a result of the marriage of local girls to G.I.s members of American and Welsh families have exchanged visits.

Pictured are some of the contributors to this story.

Lt Col William C. Burry, Commanding Colonel, MD, U.S. Army (Retired)
Officer of the 94th Medical Battalion and Mrs Virginia S. Burry November 1997

Emil C. Evancich

Evancich revisits Pontypridd with his wife Trudy in 1988. He was a member of the 94th Medical Gas Treatment Battalion and was billeted here in 1944.

Pfc Karl Gaber, Aged 20, Rhondda 1944.   *Karl Gaber, Aged 75, Bulger, Pennyslvania, 1999*

He was a member of the 186 Port Company, 187 Port Battalion U.S. Army billeted in Trherbert in May1944.

James E. Anderson home on leave in Indian prior to leaving for Europe in 1944.

James Anderson and his wife Josinah at the first 94th reunion in Petersburg, Florida in 1987.

Sgt "Andy" Anderson served with the 94th Medical Battalion. He plays an active part in the 94th Veterans Association.

A G.I. RETURNS

Frank Todaro returned to Wales in July 2000 from his home in Harrison, New York. While staying with relatives in Roch, Pembrokeshire he paid a return visit to the Rhondda and Pontypridd area accompanied by his wife Lorraine.

He commentated that the region had changed out of all recognition over the last half century. The industrial landscape associated with the coal industry had disappeared along with many buildings including their Headquarters, the former British Legion building in Pontypridd. With the construction of new roads and the general rural appearance the whole area had been transformed.

Frank Todaro and Elom Leo in 1944
Former G.I. Pfc Frank Todaro was a member of the 94th Medical Gas Treatment
Battalion billeted in Pontypridd in 1944. This photogrpah of Frank (on the right)
and his friend Elom Leo was taken in Toul, France in 1944.

Frank a life long baseball fan was a member of the 94th battalions baseball team that took part in the match in Ynysangharad Park on July 8th 1944.

Frank Torado July 2000 Frank Todaro with the author at his Penygraig home, a U.S. Army
Willys Jeep forms an appropriate background.

Many varied and interesting stories have emerged from the period when the American Army was here in the Rhondda in 1944. One of the most remarkable was the life-long friendship that occurred between Gordon Exell of Treorchy and Pfc. Arthur Bonner of New Jersey, U.S.A.

Pfc.Arthur F.Bonner in 1944

Gordon Exell and Arthur Bonner in Union, New Jersey, U.S.A. The photograph was taken in October 1985 when the Exells were visiting Arthur and Ruth Bonner to attend the wedding of their youngest daughter.

There were those American soldiers, who had been made so welcome in the Rhondda, were never to return home. Some lost their lives in the

D-Day landings on Omaha Beach. This account tells of the first memorial erected on the D-Day beaches.

AMERICANS ALL
By Dr. Daniel A. Poling

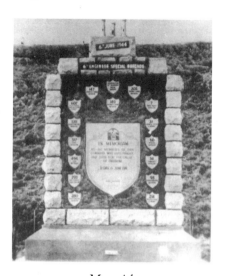

Memorial

The Normandy American National Cemetary overlooks Omaha beach. Of the 9,286 men buried here, the graves of 307 are marked: "Here rests in honored glory a comrade in arms known but to God".

It stands above the beach but still under the high bank up which they fought on D-Day, this first monument erected by Americans on French soil in World War II. I came to it by the little enclosure lower down, that bit of sacred sand where temporarily our first dead were buried. Again it was low tide, and many of the incredible obstacles they overcame were still there. Beyond were the sunken ships and barges that made a breakwater, and the remains of the improvised docks where a steady flow of troops and supplies were landed.

Already I had visited the blasted forts in Cherbourg, the twisted steel emplacements and the broken guns along that higher shore. I had seen the tunnels and the all-but-finished robot launching devices the latter pointed straight at Southampton. The Nazi genius for invention and super organisation had created the "ultimate" defenses, but there was something greater – the genius of men born free, men who would not be slaves, and who refused to live in a slave world.

And so at last I came to the monument of the 6ᵗʰ Engineers Special Brigade, which faced England looking north and west across the Channel. I read, "Designed and constructed by 147 Engineer Combat Battalion," and read the dedication; "To all members of this command who here lived and fought and died for the cause of Freedom."

I stood uncovered while a reluctant sun behind thinning storm clouds cast a shadow from the height above. There were no voices, no sounds along the beaches. The sunken vessels were a ghostly fleet.

But that shore was more alive for me than any stretch of land my feet have ever trod.

Here men "lived and fought and died" – not only to launch successfully an invasion declared to be impossible, and to liberate a continent, but to redeem their century from the sin of hate. These men are alive for evermore!

(Distributed by New York Post Syndicate)

(Extracted from The New York Post 9th March 1945)

THE AFTERMATH OF D-DAY

Newly dug graves are identified by markers bearing name, rank,
unit and serial number in a cemetery overlooking Omaha Beach.
A burial detail is carrying out its sad task on the left of the photograph.

Among the two thousand casualties on D-Day June 6ᵗʰ was a young man from Georgia Tech.4 Allen D. Shell. He and others from the 517

Port Battalion had but a few days earlier received an official welcome at Soar Chapel in Penygraig where they had been billeted.

There were to be many homes in that small mining town that would receive bad news.

This soldier was a member of the 799th Port Company of the 517 Port Battalion billeted in Penygraig in May 1944. They had been assigned to the 6th Engineer Special Brigade and had undergone special amphibious training.

They formed part of the initial assault force that landed on Omaha Beach on June 6th 1944.

When their unit left Penygraig on June 1st they took with them only their combat gear and all personal possessions and uniforms were left behind in the homes where they had been billeted.

He was billeted with Mr. and Mrs. Dando at 51, Amos Hill, Penygraig. After some time had elapsed they began to get concerned about forwarding his property to him, which included a valuable camera. Making enquiries they learned that he had been killed during the Invasion.

His mother wrote thanking them for the care they had shown her son and enclosing this photograph taken on his embarkation leave, the last photograph of them together.

This was for her and millions of others the true cost of this war.